CHUCK COLSON SPEAKS

Twelve Key Messages
from Today's Leading Defender
of the Christian Faith

CHUCK COLSON SPEAKS

Twelve Key Messages
from Today's Leading Defender
of the Christian Faith

PROMISE
PRESS

An Imprint of Barbour Publishing

Cover photography © David DeJong.

Published by Promise Press, an imprint of Barbour Publishing, Inc., P.O. Box 719, Uhrichsville, Ohio 44683, http://www.barbourbooks.com

 Member of the
Evangelical Christian
Publishers Association

Printed in the United States of America.

Table of Contents

The Enduring Revolution

The Templeton Address
University of Chicago
Chicago, Illinois
September, 1993

I speak as one transformed by Jesus Christ, the living God. He is the Way, the Truth, and the Life. He has lived in me for twenty years. His presence is the sole explanation for whatever is praiseworthy in my work, the only reason for my receiving this award (the Templeton Prize).

That is more than a statement about myself. It is a claim to truth. It is a claim that may contradict your own.

Yet on this, at least, we must agree: The right to do what I've just done—to state my faith without fear—is the first human right. Religious liberty is the essence of human dignity. We cannot build our temples on the ruins of individual conscience. For faith does not come through the weight of power, but through the hope of glory.

It is a sad fact that religious oppression is often practiced by religious groups. Sad—and inexcusable. A believer may risk prison for his own religious beliefs, but he may never build prisons for those of other beliefs.

It is our obligation—all of us here—to bring back a renewed passion for religious liberty to every nation from which we came. It is our duty to create a cultural environment where conscience can flourish. I say this for the sake of every believer imprisoned for boldness or silenced by fear. I say this for the sake of every society that has yet to learn the benefits of vital and voluntary religious faith.

The beliefs that divide us should not be minimized. But neither should the aspirations we share: for spiritual understanding; for justice and compassion; for stewardship of God's creation; for religious influence—not oppression—in the right ordering of society. And for truth against the arrogant lies of our modern age.

For at the close of this century, every religious tradition finds common ground in a common task—a struggle over the meaning and future of our world and our own particular culture. Each of us has an obligation to expose the deceptions that are incompatible with true faith.

The Four Horsemen

Four great myths define our times—the four horsemen of the present apocalypse.

The first myth is the goodness of man. The first horseman rails against heaven with the presumptuous question: Why do bad things happen to good people? He multiplies evil by denying its existence.

This myth deludes people into thinking that they are always victims, never villains; always deprived, never depraved. It dismisses responsibility as the teaching of a darker age. It can excuse any crime, because it can always blame something else—a sickness of society or a sickness of the mind.

One writer called the modern age "the golden age of exoneration." When guilt is dismissed as the illusion of narrow minds, then no one is accountable, even to his conscience.

The irony is that this should come alive in this century, of all centuries, with its gulags and death camps and killing fields. As G. K. Chesterton once said, the doctrine of original sin is the only philosophy empirically validated by the centuries of recorded human history.

It was a holocaust survivor who exposed this myth most eloquently. Yehiel Dinur was a witness during the trial of Adolf Eichmann. Dinur entered the courtroom and stared at the man behind the bulletproof glass—the man who had presided over the slaughter of millions. The court was hushed as a victim confronted a butcher.

WHEN GUILT IS DISMISSED AS THE ILLUSION OF NARROW MINDS, THEN NO ONE IS ACCOUNTABLE, EVEN TO HIS CONSCIENCE.

Then suddenly Dinur began to sob and collapsed to the floor. Not out of anger or bitterness. As he explained later in an interview, what struck him at that instant was a terrifying realization: "I was afraid about myself," Dinur said. "I saw that I am capable to do this. . . . Exactly like he."

The reporter interviewing Dinur understood precisely. "How was it possible for a man to act as Eichmann acted?" he asked. "Was he a monster? A madman? Or was he perhaps something even more terrifying. . . ? Was he normal?"

Yehiel Dinur, in a moment of chilling clarity, saw the skull beneath the skin. "Eichmann," he concluded, "is in all of us."

Jesus said it plainly: "What comes out of a man, that defiles a man" (Mark 7:20 NKJV).

The second myth of modernity is the promise of coming utopia. The second horseman arrives with sword and slaughter.

This is the myth that human nature can be perfected by government; that a new Jerusalem can be built using the tools of politics.

From the birth of this century, ruthless ideologies claimed history as their own. They moved from nation to nation on the strength of a promised utopia. They pledged to move the world but could only stain it with blood.

In communism and fascism we have seen rulers who bear the mark of Cain as a badge of honor; who pursue a savage virtue, devoid of humility and humanity. We have seen more people killed in this century by their own governments than in all its wars combined. We have seen every utopian experiment fall exhausted from the pace of its own brutality.

Yet utopian temptations persist, even in the world's democracies—stripped of their terrors perhaps, but not of their risks. The political illusion still deceives, whether it is called the great society, the new covenant, or the new world order. In each case, it promises government solutions to our deepest needs for security, peace, and meaning.

The third myth is the relativity of moral values. The third horseman sows chaos and confusion.

This myth hides the dividing line between good and evil, noble and base. It has thus created a crisis in the realm of truth. When a society abandons its transcendent values, each individual's moral vision becomes purely personal and finally equal. Society becomes merely the sum total of individual preferences, and since no preference is morally preferable, anything that can be dared will be permitted.

This leaves the moral consensus for our laws and manners in tatters. Moral neutrality slips into moral relativism. Tolerance substitutes for truth, indifference for religious conviction. And in the end, confusion undercuts all our creeds.

The fourth modern myth is radical individualism. The fourth horseman brings excess and isolation.

This myth dismisses the importance of family, church, and community; denies the value of sacrifice; and elevates individual rights and pleasures as the ultimate social value.

But with no higher principles to live by, men and women suffocate under their own expanding pleasures. Consumerism becomes empty and leveling, leaving society full of possessions but drained of ideals. This is what Vaclav Havel calls "totalitarian consumerism."

A psychologist tells the story of a despairing young woman, spent in an endless round of parties, exhausted by the pursuit of pleasure. When told she should simply stop, she responded, "You mean I don't have to do what I want to do?"

As author George MacDonald once wrote, "The one principle of hell is 'I am my own.' "

Modernity: A Case Study

I have seen firsthand the kind of society these deadly myths create. In seventeen years I have been in more prisons than I can count, in more nations than I can name. I have seen the face of the crisis of modernity in real human faces.

The myth of human goodness tells men and women they are not responsible for their actions and that everyone is a victim. "Poverty is the cause of crime," said a U.S. attorney general three decades ago. "Looters are not to blame for looting," said a U.S. president. Thus excused, millions refused accountability for their behavior. Crime soared—and is today the great plague on civilized societies.

Utopianism, however, assures us that crime can be solved by government policy. On the left, that means rehabilitation; on the right, more and tougher laws to scare people straight. But our efforts prove futile. In the past thirty years, the prison population in America has increased five-fold. Violent crime has increased just as fast.

For criminals are not made by sociological or environmental or economic forces. They are created by their own moral choices. Institutions of cold steel and bars are unable to reach the human heart, so they can neither deter nor rehabilitate.

A decade ago, social scientist James Q. Wilson searched for some correlation between crime and social forces. He discovered that in the late nineteenth century, when the nation was rapidly industrializing—conditions that should have caused crime to increase—crime actually declined. The explanation? At the time, a powerful spiritual awakening was sweeping across America, inspiring moral revival and social renewal. By contrast, in the affluent 1920s, when there should have been less economic incentive for lawlessness, crime increased. Why? In the wake of Freud and Darwin, religion fell from favor. In Wilson's words, "The educated classes began to repudiate moral uplift."

WITHOUT GOD, EVERYTHING IS PERMISSIBLE; CRIME IS INEVITABLE.

A similar study in England by Professor Christie Davies found that crime was lowest a century ago when three out of four young Britons were enrolled in Sunday school. Since then, Sunday school attendance has declined, and crime has correspondingly increased.

Crime is a mirror of a community's moral state. A society cannot long survive if the demands of human dignity are not written on our hearts. No number of police can enforce order; no threat of punishment can create it. Crime and violence frustrate every political answer, because there can be no solution apart from character and creed.

But relativism and individualism have undermined the traditional beliefs that once informed our character and defined our creed. There are no standards to guide us. Dostoyevsky's diagnosis was correct: Without God, everything is permissible; crime is inevitable.

These myths constitute a threat for all of us, regardless of our culture or the faith communities we represent. The four horsemen of the present apocalypse lead away from the cloud and fire of God's presence into a barren wilderness. Modernity was once judged by the heights of its aspirations. Today it must be judged by the depth of its decadence. That decadence has marked the West most deeply; this makes it imperative that we understand the struggle for the soul of Western civilization.

The Paradox of Our Times

We stand at a pivotal moment in history, when nations around the world are looking westward. In the past five years, the balance of world power shifted dramatically. Suddenly, remarkably, almost inexplicably, one of history's most sustained assaults on freedom collapsed before our eyes.

The world has been changed, not through the militant dialectic of communism, but through the power of unarmed truth. It found revolution in the highest hopes of common men. Love of liberty steeled under the weight of tyranny; the path of the future was charted in prison cells.

This revolution's symbolic moment was May Day 1990. Protesters followed the tanks, missiles, and troops rumbling across Red Square. One, a bearded Orthodox monk, darted under the reviewing stand where Gorbachev and other Soviet leaders stood. He thrust a huge crucifix into the air, shouting above the crowd, "Mikhail Sergeyevich! Christ is risen!"

Gorbachev turned and walked off the platform.

Across a continent the signal went. In defiant hope, a spell was broken. The lies of decades were exposed. Fear and terror fled. And millions awoke as from a long nightmare.

Their waking dream is a world revolution. Almost overnight the Western model of economic, political, and social liberty has captured the imagination of reformers and given hope to the oppressed. We saw it at Tiananmen Square, where a replica of the Statue of Liberty, an icon of Western freedom, became a symbol of Chinese hope. We saw it in Czechoslovakia when a worker stood before a desolate factory and read to a crowd, with tears in his eyes, the American Declaration of Independence.

This is one of history's defining moments. The faults of the West are evident—but equally evident are the extraordinary gifts it has to offer the world. The gift of markets that increase living standards and choices. The gift of political institutions where power flows from the consent of the governed, not the barrel of a gun. The gift of social beliefs that encourage tolerance and individual autonomy.

Free markets. Free governments. Free minds.

But just at this moment, after the struggle of this century. . .just at this moment, with a new era of liberty our realistic hope. . .just at this moment, the culture that fashioned this freedom is being overrun by the four horsemen. It has embraced the destructive myths of modernity, which are poisoning its wellspring of justice and virtue and stripping away its most essential humanizing, civilizing influence.

Roots of the Western Ideal

Make no mistake: This humanizing, civilizing influence is the Judeo-Christian heritage. It is a heritage brought to life anew in each generation by men and women whose lives are transformed by the living God and filled with holy conviction.

Despite the failures of some of its followers—the crusades and inquisitions—this heritage has laid the foundations of freedom in the West. It has established a standard of justice over both men and nations. It has proclaimed a higher law that exposes the pretensions of tyrants. It has taught that every human soul is on a path of immortality, that every man and woman is to be treated as the child of a King.

This muscular faith has motivated excellence in art and discovery in science. It has undergirded an ethic of work and an ethic of service. It has tempered freedom with internal restraint, so our laws could be permissive while our society was not.

THE FAULTS OF THE WEST ARE EVIDENT— BUT EQUALLY EVIDENT ARE THE EXTRAORDINARY GIFTS IT HAS TO OFFER THE WORLD.

Christian conviction inspires public virtue, the moral impulse to do good. It has sent legions into battle against disease, oppression, and bigotry. It ended the slave trade, built hospitals and orphanages, and tamed the brutality of mental wards and prisons.

In every age it has given divine mercy a human face in the lives of those who follow Christ—from Francis of Assisi to the great social reformers Wilberforce and Shaftesbury to Mother Teresa to the tens of thousands of Prison Fellowship volunteers who take hope to the captives—and who are the true recipients of this award.

Christian conviction also shapes personal virtue, the moral imperative to be good. It subdues an obstinate will. It ties a tether to self-interest and violence.

Finally, Christian conviction provides a principled belief in human freedom. As Lord Acton explained, "Liberty is the highest political end of man. . . . [But] no country can be free without religion. It creates and strengthens the notion of duty. If men are not kept straight by duty, they must be by fear. The more they are kept by fear, the less they are free. The greater the strength of duty, the greater the liberty."

The kind of duty to which Acton refers is driven by the most compelling motivation. I and every other Christian have experienced it. It is the duty that flows from gratitude to God that He would send His only Son to die so we might live.

The Four Horsemen in the West

This is the lesson of centuries: that ordered liberty is one of faith's triumphs. And yet, Western cultural and political elites seem blinded by modernity's myths to the historic civilizing role of Christian faith. And so, in the guise of pluralism and tolerance, they have set about to exile religion from our common life. They use the power of the media and the law like steel wool to scrub public debates and public places bare of religious ideas and symbols. But what is left is sterile and featureless and cold.

These elites seek freedom without self-restraint, liberty without standards. But they find instead the revenge of offended absolutes.

Courts strike down even perfunctory prayers, and we are surprised that schools, bristling with barbed wire, look more like prisons than prisons do.

Universities reject the very idea of truth, and we are shocked when the best and the brightest of their graduates loot and betray.

Celebrities mock the traditional family, even revile it as a form of slavery, and we are appalled at the human tragedy of broken homes and millions of unwed mothers.

The media celebrate sex without responsibility, and we are

horrified by sexual plagues.

Our lawmakers justify the taking of innocent life in sterile clinics, and we are terrorized by the disregard for life in blood-soaked streets.

C. S. Lewis described this irony a generation ago. "We laugh at honor," he said, "and are shocked to find traitors in our midst. . . . We castrate and bid the geldings be fruitful."

A generation of cultural leaders wants to live off the spiritual capital of its inheritance, while denigrating the ideals of its ancestors. It squanders a treasure it no longer values. It celebrates its liberation when it should be trembling for its future.

The Path to Tyranny

Where does the stampede of the four horsemen lead us? Only one place: tyranny. A new kind of cultural tyranny that finds minds, uninformed by traditions and standards, easy to shape.

Philosopher Hannah Arendt described totalitarianism as a process where lonely, rootless individuals, deprived of meaning and community, welcome the captivity of ideology. To escape their inner emptiness, they seek out new forms of servitude. Trading independence for security, they blend into faceless conformity.

The lonely crowd always finds a leader. It submits to the party line and calls it freedom. America is filled with willing recruits to follow a new Grand Inquisitor.

This coming cultural tyranny already casts its shadow across university campuses where repressive speech codes stifle free debate; across courthouses and legislatures where officials hunt down and purge every religious symbol; across network newsrooms and board rooms where nothing is censored except traditional belief. Our modern elites speak of enlightened tolerance while preparing shackles for those who disagree. This is what Chesterton defined as true bigotry: "the anger of men who have no convictions."

Disdaining the past and its values, we flee the judgment of the dead. We tear down memory's monuments—removing every guidepost and landmark—and wander in unfamiliar country. But it is a sterile wasteland in which men and women are left with carefully furnished lives and utterly barren souls.

And so, paradoxically, at the very moment much of the rest of the world seems to be reaching out for Western liberal ideas, the West itself, beguiled by myths of modernity, is undermining the very foundation of those ideals.

This is irony without humor; farce without joy. Western elites are carefully separating the wheat from the chaff and keeping the chaff. They are performing a modern miracle of turning wine into water.

This crisis is not only alarming, it is also urgent. In earlier times, social patterns were formed over centuries by tradition and intellectual debate, then gradually filtered to the masses. Now, through technology, a social revolution can be wired directly to the brain. It comes through satellites and videos, through pleasing images and catchy tunes. Refugees on a boat from southern China were recently intercepted by the U.S. Coast Guard. Their entire knowledge of the English language consisted of one acronym—"MTV."

The world's newly developing nations are in a revolution of rising expectations that may become a trap of misplaced hope. Nations that import a Western ideal stripped of its soul will find only what we have found: pleasures as shallow as the moment, emptiness as deep as eternity.

The Contemporary Challenge

I say to you assembled here today from every part of the globe that this is a challenge facing all of us. At this extraordinary moment in world history, many nations once enslaved to ruthless ideologies have now been set free only to face a momentous decision: Each must decide whether to embrace the myths of modernity or turn to a deeper, older tradition, the half-forgotten teachings of saints and sages.

I say to my compatriots in the West that we bear a particular responsibility—for modernity's myths have found fertile soil in our lands, and we have offered haven to the four horsemen who trample the dreams and hopes of men and women everywhere. As the world looks to us, let us summon the courage to challenge our comfortable assumptions, to scrutinize the effect we have on our global neighbors. . .and then to recover that which has been the very soul and conscience of our own civilization.

For the West today is like Janus, with a two-sided face—one offering futility, empty secularism, and death; the other offering freedom, rich, biblically rooted spirituality, and life. Commentators have described the internal conflict between these two as a culture war. Some have even declared the war over. The four horsemen, they tell us, are the victors at this chapter in our history.

BY THE CROSS HE OFFERS HOPE, BY THE RESURRECTION HE ASSURES HIS TRIUMPH.

The Enduring Revolution

Admittedly the signs are not auspicious, as I have been at pains to show, and it is easy to become discouraged. But a Christian has neither the reason nor the right. For history's cadence is called with a confident voice. The God of Abraham, Isaac, and Jacob reigns. His plan and purpose rob the future of its fears.

By the Cross He offers hope, by the Resurrection He assures His triumph. This cannot be resisted or delayed. Mankind's only choice is to recognize Him now or in the moment of ultimate judgment.

Our only decision is to welcome His rule or to fear it.

But this gives everyone hope. For this is a vision beyond a vain utopia or a timid new world order. It is the vision of an Enduring Revolution. One that breaks more than the chains of tyranny; it breaks the chains of sin and death. And it proclaims a liberation that the cruelest prison cannot contain.

The Templeton Prize is awarded for progress in religion. In a technological age, we often equate progress with breaking through barriers in science and knowledge. But progress does not always mean discovering something new. Sometimes it means rediscovering wisdom that is ancient and eternal. Sometimes, in our search for advancement, we find it only where we began. The greatest progress in religion today is to meet every nation's most urgent need: A revolution that begins in the human heart. It is the Enduring Revolution.

In the aftermath of the tragedy in Waco, Texas, and terrorist bombings in New York, we heard dire warnings, even from the president of the United States, of religious extremism. But that, with due respect, is not the world's gravest threat. Far more dangerous is the decline of true religion and of its humanizing values in our daily lives. No ideology—not even liberal democracy—is sufficient. Every noble hope is empty apart from the Enduring Revolution.

This revolution reaches across centuries and beyond politics. It confounds the ambitions of kings, and rewards the faith of a child. It clothes itself in the rags of common lives, then emerges with sudden splendor. It violates every jaded expectation with the paradox of its power.

The evidence of its power is humility. The evidence of its conquest is peace. The evidence of its triumph is service. But that still, small voice of humility, of peace, of service becomes a thundering judgment that shakes every human institution to its foundation.

The Enduring Revolution teaches that freedom is found in

submission to a moral law. It says that duty is our sharpest weapon against fear and tyranny. This revolution raises an unchanging and eternal moral standard—and offers hope to everyone who fails to reach it. This revolution sets the content of justice—and transforms the will to achieve it. It builds communities of character—and of compassion.

On occasion, God provides glimpses of this glory. I witnessed one in an unlikely place: a prison in Brazil like none I've ever seen.

Twenty years ago in the city of San Jose dos Campos, a prison was turned over to two Christian laymen. They called it Humaita, and their plan was to run it on Christian principles.

The prison has only two full-time staff; the rest of the work is done by inmates. Every prisoner is assigned another inmate to whom he is accountable. In addition, every prisoner is assigned a volunteer family from the outside that works with him during his term and after his release. Every prisoner joins a chapel program or else takes a course in character development.

When I visited Humaita, I found the inmates smiling—particularly the murderer who held the keys, opened the gates, and let me in. Wherever I walked, I saw men at peace. I saw clean living areas. I saw people working industriously. The walls were decorated with biblical sayings from Psalms and Proverbs.

Humaita has an astonishing record. Its recidivism rate is 4 percent compared to 75 percent in the rest of Brazil and the United States. How is that possible?

I saw the answer when my inmate guide escorted me to the notorious punishment cell once used for torture. Today, he told me, that block houses only a single inmate. As we reached the end of the long concrete corridor and he put the key into the lock, he paused and asked, "Are you sure you want to go in?"

"Of course," I replied impatiently. "I've been in isolation cells all over the world." Slowly he swung open the massive door, and I saw the prisoner in that punishment cell: a crucifix, beautifully carved by the Humaita inmates—the prisoner Jesus, hanging on the cross.

"He's doing time for all the rest of us," my guide said softly.

In that cross carved by loving hands is a holy subversion. It heralds change more radical than mankind's most fevered dreams. Its followers expand the boundaries of a kingdom that can never fail. A shining kingdom that reaches into the darkest corners of every community into the darkest corners of every mind. A kingdom of deathless hope, of restless virtue, of endless peace.

This work proceeds, this hope remains, this fire will not be quenched: The Enduring Revolution of the Cross of Christ.

The Prisoner

Chuck's Annual
In-Prison Easter Sermon

The prisoner said nothing as people shouted charges against Him. He had been roughly pushed from cell to cell and questioned throughout the long night. His body hurt, but He stood straight before His accusers.

He knew what it was to be alone. Many people hated Him. One of His closest friends had become a snitch and turned Him in. Then the long night of abuse. Now He stood before the governor, the man who could set Him free with one stroke of his pen.

The governor tapped his fingers on his desk as he spoke to the man's accusers: "Why are you pressing charges against this man? He doesn't belong in my courtroom. Try Him yourselves!"

"We don't have the authority," they said. "You judge Him."

The governor sighed. He could see that the man was innocent. But the prisoner did have an odd way of speaking—when He spoke. For the most part, He kept silent, and the governor was not comfortable with silence.

The prisoner's trial had now become public. A restless crowd lined the fences of the governor's mansion. The governor, always aware of his public image, tuned in to the crowd's mood. He offered the prisoner a chance to plea-bargain, but the man would not lie in order to save Himself. He looked steadily at the governor. "I was born, and now live, to bear witness to the truth," He said. The words sounded strange in that room of deals and copping pleas. The governor shook his head. "Truth," he said tiredly. "What is truth?"

He turned to the angry crowd pressing against the gates. "Make your deals!" they cried. "Release another prisoner, but not this man! Execute Him!" They screamed until their voices gave out. They were like a pack of dogs barking for fresh blood.

The governor shrugged. The mob grew quiet as he stood to speak. "I personally find this man not guilty," he said. "He has committed no crime and certainly doesn't deserve the death penalty.

"But He's your business, not mine. By the power vested in me, I sentence Him to death—today." The air was still for a moment, then filled with cheers. The governor's public image was safe.

The guards sprang forward and tightened the bonds of the condemned man. Then they led Him from the governor's palace to a cold cell on death row. They ripped off His clothes and strip-searched Him and beat Him with nail-studded whips until His back was a mass of bloody flesh. Then they forced Him to the place of execution, a hilltop outside of town at a well-traveled crossroads. They laid Jesus, the prisoner, on a rough wooden cross. Blood flowed from His hands and feet as the guards pounded spikes through them into the hard wood. To the jeers of the onlookers, the cross was lifted into the air. It stood dark and ugly against the morning sky.

People for miles around saw Him suffer. They were old hands at such executions. They knew what would follow: He would hang there for hours slowly dying as the blood drained from His body. It was terrible pain but proper punishment for One who claimed He was God.

Two convicted thieves hung on crosses on either side of Him, also in pain. One angrily cursed Jesus: "Aren't You the Christ? Save Yourself and us!" The other criminal understood what the first did not and rebuked him: "Don't you fear God? We were condemned fairly—we are guilty. But this man has done nothing wrong." Even though he was in pain, his mind was clear. He believed that this man hanging next to him could forgive his sins. "Jesus," he cried out, "remember me when You come into Your kingdom!" Jesus turned toward him, "Today you will be with Me in Paradise."

YES, JESUS CHRIST, THE INNOCENT PRISONER, LIVES TODAY.

The blood continued to flow from Christ's ragged wounds, His breathing grew labored, then shallow, then stopped. After hours of agony, the ordeal was over—He was dead.

That horrible execution took place two thousand years ago. But the execution was not the end. That same prisoner, condemned and killed for claiming He was God, proved His claims were true. Three days later, fulfilling the Bible's prophecy, He rose from the dead. He walked and talked with His disciples again. More than five hundred eyewitnesses saw Him alive during a forty-day period. Then He returned to heaven, where He rules today with God the Father. Yes, Jesus Christ, the innocent prisoner, lives today.

The fact gives hope and meaning to every person who has ever been accused and condemned, whether justly or unjustly. We have all done wrong; we have all fallen short of what God wants for us. What does He want? A personal relationship with each of us. He wants to know us—and He wants us to know Him. And nothing we or others have done can prevent Him from knowing us.

If you are a prisoner, this man Jesus knows what you are going through. Millions of comfortable, respectable people don't know what it is like to be cut off from the world, to hurt inside, to suffer the pain of prison. But Jesus does. Jesus has been where you are today.

Do you think that Christ can be found only in beautiful churches? History shows that He walked on dusty roads; He laughed with friends; He knew pain and sorrow. He wasn't a member of the high society. He owned nothing. He was born in a borrowed manger, rode a borrowed donkey, and was buried in a borrowed tomb.

Most of His friends were losers—prostitutes, loudmouths, poor fishermen, and criminals. He touched the eyes of blind men and they saw; He spoke to the crippled and they threw away their crutches. He lived among the poor and comforted the oppressed. He saw through the political games and phony lives of the religious people of His day.

In the end, these so-called religious people did Him in because He cared for the poor, the downtrodden, the prisoners, and they didn't. He exposed them as fakes. They did not want to see the ugly sores in society. They did not want to hear the heart-breaking cries of the hurting. They did not want to face the rejects and outcasts. They killed Him because He wouldn't let them claim to love God and forget human need.

But Jesus' love was real. His love was tough enough to give everything. He died as a prisoner in order to overcome death for the rest of us. He became like us so that we could become like Him— righteous before God.

You can be like that first thief next to Jesus, complaining angrily to God, mocking Jesus. Or you can be like the second thief. You can recognize Jesus for who He is, the holy Son of God. You can admit that you are sinful and guilty and ask Him to be your Savior.

Think about it when you are alone tonight—maybe in your cell or walking across the prison yard. If you're like the second thief, then Jesus makes the same promise to you that He did to him. You can be with Him—right now. That prisoner, Jesus, will be in your cell with His hand on you. He will make you God's own son or daughter. At that moment, a new life begins for you.

This is the gospel. It seems like a failure; it is the opposite of what the rich and powerful expect. Yet over the past two thousand years, millions from every nation and walk of life, from prison cells to the White House, have recognized that Jesus Christ is God. Jesus the prisoner lives today. Only He can set the rest of us prisoners free.

Can We Be Good Without God?

King College
Bristol, Tennessee
Commencement, 1995

Can we be good without God? That is the age-old question so pointedly asked by Dostoevsky in his novel *Brothers Karamazov*. It raises a question you need to consider in a personal way: "What is it that causes you to seek a good—or virtuous—life?"

I would say the answer to that question boils down to one word. . .an old-fashioned word that you don't hear much in American discourse today. It's four letters. The word is duty. Duty—both your civic duty as a citizen and, more important, your Christian duty. It is critical to your character, critical to your country, and critical to your role in the kingdom of God.

Forgiven by God

On August 12, 1973, in the midst of the darkest days of Watergate, out of the White House office and visiting a friend of mine outside of Boston, I heard the gospel for the first time. That night, in a flood of tears, I surrendered my life to Christ. Nothing has been the same since; nothing can ever be the same again.

On the twentieth anniversary of my conversion, I went to a very favorite place of mine on the shore. I looked out over the sea, and I reflected on those two decades as a Christian, on the extraordinary things God has done with my life. I reflected on my coming out of prison, a broken man, and my starting a ministry that works in prisons all over the world—far beyond anything I ever could have planned; it is the work of a sovereign God. I reflected on winning the Templeton Prize, one of the most prestigious honors one could receive, and going to Buckingham Palace to accept the prize and speaking in Parliament. I considered the books, the honorary degrees, the heads of states I have met around the world, some of them having converted to Christ through reading books I've written. There on the shore, I thought about all of those things. You might say I piled up stones of remembrance. When Joshua took the children of Israel across the Jordan, he piled stones to mark the place of crossing, because he wanted people always to remember what God had done in that place. At the seaside I mentally piled up my little stones of remembrance of what God had done in my life. And the brightest, shiniest stone of all was my memory of the moment I was converted and knew for a fact that I had been forgiven of my sins by Christ's atoning death on the Cross. In the hymn writer Charles Wesley's words: "His blood availed for me."

I think of the comment by Karl Barth, one of the great theologians of the twentieth century. As an older man, he was asked to summarize the greatest theological truth he had ever learned. He said, "Jesus loves me, this I know, for the Bible tells me so."

Twenty years after finding Christ, I could look at myself and know that I could live because Christ had died for my sins—not the "Watergate" sins you read about in history books, because I didn't do anything at Watergate that the Democrats hadn't done before me. You read about those terrible dirty tricks that I was accused of, but they are nothing compared to the sins I know buried in this heart. I stand amazed to think that the Son of God was nailed to the Cross and suffered the most agonizing painful death to take upon Himself my sins so that I might be forgiven. If I did not know that, honestly, I could not live with myself.

Albert Camus, one of the fathers of modern existentialism, whose books have poisoned American thought since the sixties, believed there was no God. Camus lived for the moment. He believed one overcame the "nothingness of life" by heroic individualism. He said, "There is only one philosophical question in life: suicide." If you can't be forgiven, you either have to kill your conscience or kill yourself, if you are honest.

> I STAND AMAZED TO THINK THAT THE SON OF GOD. . . SUFFERED THE MOST AGONIZING PAINFUL DEATH TO TAKE UPON HIMSELF MY SINS SO THAT I MIGHT BE FORGIVEN.

No! Nothing, nothing compares to the substitutionary atonement, because Jesus Christ, the Son of God, died for your sins on that Cross. There is nothing comparable. And when you think about it, it has to inspire within you a sense of gratitude, the deepest kind of gratitude.

Driven by Gratitude

Think about what gratitude means. Hebrews 12:28 says, because we receive a kingdom which cannot be shaken, "let us show gratitude, by which we may offer to God an acceptable service with reverence and awe" (NASB). All of my life I have been grateful for things. The grandson of humble immigrants, I was grateful that I got a scholarship to college, when I couldn't have gone otherwise. I was very grateful to Brown University which educated me. I was grateful to my family for their sacrifice on my behalf. I was grateful to this country. I was grateful to the U.S. Marine Corps, which took a flabby college kid and turned him into a man. I was grateful to Richard Nixon. I went to his funeral, and I was one of the few guys who could walk in with his head up, because I had never said anything in all of those twenty years critical of Richard Nixon. I served him; I admired him. He was my friend, and right to his dying day, I remained his friend. I was and am grateful to our country, for our forefathers who died so that we might have the freedoms we have today. That gratitude makes us good citizens.

But if you are grateful for those things—and think about the things in your own life for which you are grateful—how much more grateful are you that you have been forgiven of your sins, that in Christ you are free indeed, a child and friend of God?

What does that kind of gratitude do? If you really understand that gratitude, it gives you a sense of duty, as the writer of Hebrews says, to live your life in ways that provide acceptable service to your Lord out of gratitude for what He has done for you.

I was in Czechoslovakia a few years ago, and I wanted to meet one man more than any other. His name was Vaclav Maly. He was the Catholic priest who in 1981 had been defrocked for preaching the gospel and dispatched by the Communists to clean the toilets in the subway system of Prague. But on Christmas Eve, 1989, when the crowds began to move out into the streets, when it looked like, finally, the Communist behemoth was to be overturned, the crowd started chanting, "Maly! Maly!" Up out of the subway came Vaclav Maly, the defrocked priest. He led them down to the main square of old Prague, and, as the *New York Times* wrote, eight hundred thousand people gathered around while Maly administered a service and offered forgiveness to all the Communists. All they had to do was come forward and repent. They did by the hundreds! The next morning, the tanks were gone. It was the velvet revolution; not a single drop of blood was shed. Maly was the hero of the velvet revolution.

Vaclav Havel, who became president of the country, called Maly in one day and said, "Father Maly, you can be anything you want in this government, from prime minister on down." Maly said, "Oh no! I just want to preach the gospel. I just want to tell people about Jesus." And so he went back to his church.

When I visited there in 1991, I wanted to meet him. I went to the Reform pastor who was my host and said, "Do you happen to know Vaclav Maly?"

He said, "Everybody in Czechoslovakia knows him, but I know him because we pray together every week for thirty minutes."

And so he took me to Maly's house. It was a little, gray, grubby building on the outskirts of Prague up on the side of a hill. There were five mailboxes and buttons, and one said, "V. Maly." Here he was, one of the most famous men in the world—"V. Maly." I pressed the button, and down to the front door came this man about forty years old. His face might have been chiseled out by Michelangelo, framed in beautiful, curly black hair, and with a wonderful, radiant smile. Within seconds we were embracing. Then I went up into his little apartment—a tiny little place shared with his father. On the table was mail from all over the world, and the telephone rang constantly. Nevertheless, we sat and had the most wonderful forty-five minutes of fellowship.

As I left, I turned and said, "I want you to know what a hero you are to many of us in the West."

His answer to me has changed my view of Christian service ever since. He said, "Oh no, Chuck! I am not a hero. A hero is someone who does something he doesn't have to do. I was simply doing my duty."

This concept sadly is not understood in our society today. We have lost the sense of duty. We have lost it as citizens. Princeton students, when the registration for the draft was reinstated, went parading around with a big sign, "Nothing is worth dying for." If nothing is worth dying for, nothing is worth living for. Forty percent of the baby boomers said that they wouldn't serve their country if their country were in danger, because they don't feel it is their responsibility.

THE ROOT OF DUTY IS GRATITUDE FOR WHAT YOU HAVE BEEN GIVEN.

I offer this illustration, hoping it is understood, as intended, in a nonpartisan spirit. I mean nothing invidious about this from a political perspective. Maybe the best example of the mistaken view of duty we have in our culture today was when President Clinton in 1993 went to the Vietnam Memorial, after having refused to serve in the Vietnam War. Maybe you remember the controversy. It took courage on the president's part to face that crowd. Vietnam veterans said that they would protest, and they did when he arrived at the Vietnam Memorial. I watched this on television, and, as a former marine captain, it was a very sad day for me. The president of the United States stood in front of 250 veterans who did an about-face and turned their backs on their commander in chief. They just stood there with their backs toward him. This saddened me greatly.

But then the president said: "Some have suggested that it is wrong for me to be here today because I did not agree a quarter of a century ago with the decision to send young men and women to battle in Vietnam." The vets booed. There had been silent protest up to that point, but at that moment the whole crowd went wild. They understood what the president didn't. He didn't get it! He didn't go to war because he thought the war was immoral; they may have thought the war was immoral, too, but they went because it was their duty. Our society needs to understand that out of gratitude for what our forefathers have done for us, shedding their blood so that we might live in freedom, we do our duty, sometimes regardless of judgments about whether we like it or don't like it. President Clinton missed the point.

Much of our generation today misses the point: The root of duty is gratitude for what you have been given. It is the heart of personal character. It is knowing what you ought to do and making it more important than what you want to do.

I think of a prayer prayed by John McCain, senator from Arizona. During the Vietnam War, John's father was commander in chief of the Pacific Fleet and a great, personal friend of mine. When John McCain's plane went down in Vietnam, my heart was broken because I knew him well, and his dad and I were so close. To think that this young man was in the Hanoi Hilton, in a bamboo cage, being tortured! I thought about him every day that I was in the White House. When John McCain was in Vietnam, he was not able to walk without crutches and weighed about a hundred pounds. He prayed, not to be free but for strength. His captors offered to release him, but this was his response, written for *Life* magazine:

The way we got into prison wasn't because of God. It was because we were rending unto Caesar what was Caesar's because our countries were at war. It wasn't right to ask God to free me. I thought I should leave that situation only if it were in the best interest of my country. In 1968, the Vietnamese offered me the opportunity to go home. I had a broken arm, and a knee I couldn't walk on without crutches, and I weighed about one hundred pounds. I wanted to go home more than almost anything in the world, but our code of conduct says the sick and injured go home in order of capture, and there were others who had been there longer. I knew they wanted to release me because my father was Commander of U.S. Forces in the Pacific. It would have given them a propaganda victory. I prayed for the strength to make the right decision, and I am certain those prayers have helped me do what I had to do. I had to stay there.

Duty is doing what we have to do and ought to do, not what we want to do. What does this mean to us? It means as citizens, we are going to be the best of citizens! There is a real breakdown of civic virtue in our culture today, and it is because so many people have lost the sense of gratitude and the sense of duty that flows from it. Augustine once said that the Christian is the best of citizens because the Christian does out of the love of God what others do only because they are required by law.

Tocqueville is often quoted for what he said about America when he visited here in the nineteenth century. He was struck by our churches, yes, our liberty, yes, our freedom, but more than anything else he was struck by the American sense of community, civic virtue, and people doing their duty. He said there weren't ten men in all of France who do what Americans do every day as a matter of routine—we care for one another. The heart of what our Republican founders called "civic virtue and civic duty" is in caring for our neighbors, which we, as Christians, understand above all and should model as exemplary citizens. As Christians, our duty is inspired by gratitude to God for what He has done; that is the very heart of the Christian life. All to Him I owe!

Restrained by Truth or Tyranny

The consecrated, dutiful life—What does it mean?

First, it means being obedient to the Holy Scriptures and living the way God commands. Before this day is over, before the sun sets, you will be tempted at least three times to do something contrary to what God teaches. Condition yourself. Think constantly about the truth of God's revelation, so much so that it becomes habitual to react in the Christian, biblical manner.

Second, it means rightly ordering your personal priorities. I haven't done a very good job of this in my own life. I used to think the most important thing was getting ahead—success, power, and achievement. I didn't realize that a right order of priorities is to love God and to love your family and then turn your attention to the work God has called you to.

Third, the faithful Christian life of duty means seeing what you are doing in life as a calling from God. I don't care whether you are a banker or a lawyer. I don't care what your profession is—it could be sweeping floors. You do it to the glory of God, as Martin Luther said, because it is your vocation. It's the way in which you witness.

Fourth, "Let this mind be in you, which was also in Christ Jesus" (Phil. 2:5 KJV). With all humility, with gentleness and reverence, think Christianly about every single aspect of life. I cannot describe the discouragement I felt one day when lecturing to three hundred people, most of them Christians, many of them regularly attending a Sunday school class in my own church. When we got to the seventh talk of the series, I said, "This lecture today is going to be on Christian world view. You know what a biblical world view is, don't you?" Of three hundred people, only three raised hands!

I continued, "I mean a view of all of life informed by scriptural truth. What does Scripture tell us about literature and art and science and medicine and bioethics and all the issues today, politics being only one of many? We think it is the only one, but it isn't. How many are familiar with this?" And then about six or seven hands went up.

I said, "Have you ever heard that we are to take every thought captive in obedience to Christ? What does that mean? It means we ought to look at all of life and measure it in the light of Christian truth so that we can defend truth in the age in which we live."

Make no mistake; there is a collision of world views. We are living on the cusp, on the edge of a collision of two views of life. One view says there is no ultimate reality, there is no meaning, there is no purpose, everything is relative, there are no absolutes. The other says God is, He is not silent, He is in His heaven, there is ultimate meaning, and it is in God. Those two world views are colliding, and you as educated Christian people are going to be combatants; you are going to be coming in contact with educated secular people. And your job is to show them how Christians think as Christians about music, literature, popular culture, science, medicine, politics, anthropology, sociology. In every aspect of life you are to think Christianly.

Why is it so important today? I work in the criminal justice area, and we are at a very dangerous time in American life. Debate in the aftermath of the Oklahoma City bombing of a federal building centers around the question, "Is it right to criticize government?" People are missing the point; the criticism is not of the government, it is of the people who are in the government—the ruling class that has set itself apart from the people. That is where the real criticism is. But you are going to see a great debate churn in American life over the next years over the question, "What is permissible dissent?" What are we able to say and do?

On many campuses today, the politically correct stance says, "You can't say anything if it impinges on someone else's right to believe anything that person wants to believe." Dissent from the politically acceptable view is stifled. That restrictive mind-set is going to tighten and affect all of American life. And if society experiences social stress, those pressures will lead to more government authority and more restrictions on individual freedom.

IF THERE IS NOT SOME SENSE OF DUTY, PARTICULARLY THAT INSPIRED BY RELIGIOUS CONVICTIONS, THEN THE STATE BEGINS TO IMPOSE ITS POWER.

Think what can happen as crime gets worse in our society. By the year 2005, the number of fourteen- to seventeen-year-old young people in the U.S. population will be 26 percent higher than it is today, and that age group is known to be the most crime prone. Most random, senseless shootings are done by kids—teens—who take a gun and blow people away for the fun of it. Or they settle an argument over a jacket with a gun. That is going to get worse; it is a demographic time bomb. Faced with unsafe streets, the reactions of Americans will be, "Give me order at any price!"

You see, this collision of world views is not just some academic, intellectual exercise. It is an issue over what kind of society we live in. If there is not some sense of duty, particularly that inspired by religious convictions, then the state begins to impose its power.

We are only beginning to see what will be an emerging debate over tyranny in American life. In Dade County, Florida, a poll recently indicated that 74 percent of the people would be willing to give up their civil liberties, give up their Fourth Amendment right against unreasonable search and seizure, in the interest of reducing crime in Miami. Across the country, there are 1,100 jurisdictions with curfews, which is nothing short of marshal law. As the debate escalates over the proper response to crime, we Christians must know the issues; we must be able to articulate a Christian world view and defend the truth in the marketplace of ideas.

Why is duty so important? More than a hundred years ago, Lord Acton understood it. He gave us a pithy little proverb: "Power corrupts; absolute power corrupts absolutely." You all know that. Everybody knows that in every civics class in America. Lord Acton said many things that were far more important; talking about absolute power, for instance, he said: "Liberty is the highest political end of man, but no country can be free without religion."

Can man be good without God? That is, can we have a free and virtuous citizenry? The answer is not without God. No country can be free without religion, for it creates and strengthens the notion of duty. And the individual desire to be good is essential to preserve freedom. Lord Acton again put it well: "If people are not kept straight by duty, they must be kept by fear. The more they are kept by fear, the less they are free. The greater the strength of duty; the greater the liberty."

Call it Colson's law, if you want but, depraved beings that we are, there are only two restraints against irresponsible antisocial human behavior: One is here in our own hearts; one is out there—the police. You take away the internal restraints of the heart and conscience, and you are controlled by force. Take away a nation's Bibles; polish up the bayonets.

The great crisis of our hour is whether our citizens understand that we have a duty to civic virtue that arises from gratitude for our national heritage and whether Christians understand that we have a duty to our God out of gratitude for what He did in sending His Son to die for our sins. That is the main line of defense against the encroaching forces of tyranny. And it is the main line of defense that you must maintain in the coming years.

Do your duty as citizens and as Christians. Be thinking men and women who can give a reason for the hope that is within you, always with gentleness and reverence. Be obedient to the Word. Care about widows and orphans. Care about justice. Defend the truth. Do your duty, and you will be better people for it. Liberty in our land will be strengthened, and the kingdom of God will be glorified. God bless you.

The Great Hope
for the New Millennium

Gaither Praise Gathering
Indianapolis, Indiana
November, 1998

We're facing the turn of the millennium—a most historic moment. What does the event mean? It marks two thousand years since the birth of Christ. The whole world is getting ready to celebrate the birth of our Lord. And Christians, of all people, ought to be jubilant and excited and upbeat and celebratory over what's about to happen.

Think of it! The most influential person in all of human history was the son of a carpenter. Despised, He died on a cross marked with a sign that mocked Him as the King of the Jews. And two thousand years later, we celebrate His birth and life.

Yet everywhere I go lately, I discover that the church—the Evangelical church at least—is sensing despair, almost a malaise rather than celebration. One can, I suppose, understand why. We look at what's happening in politics. We see the scandals, not only in the White House, but also with special-interests buying out the Congress on both sides of the political aisle. And we look at the voters, and they don't seem to care. One by one, we seem to be losing the battles of the culture war.

In recent elections, both Colorado and Washington State put referenda on the ballots to ban partial-birth abortion. I can't imagine being in favor of crushing a baby's skull in the birth canal. And yet the voters of those two states voted down a ban on partial-birth abortion, even though 70 percent of the people in the state said they opposed the process. It's like we have been seized by an absolute libertarianism: We don't want government telling us what to do about anything. And I just came from Minnesota, where they elected a professional wrestler as governor as a way of saying, "We don't care about your politicians. We're going to do it our way." There's almost an antihero complex in our culture.

And we see Christians being blamed for everything. I turn on the television set and here's Katie Couric blaming Jim Dobson and the rest of us for the brutal murder of Matthew Shepherd in Wyoming. Incredible! If anything goes wrong in life, it's the Christians who are blamed. So it's understandable why there's this temptation to despair.

And the courts deciding religious liberty cases seem consistently over the last ten years to rule against us, including the *Boerne v. Flores* case, which struck down the Religious Freedom Restoration Act. As a result, the most serious threat to religious liberty in American history is going on right now—a battle raging in the Congress.

So for Christians, it's understandable why there'd be this temptation to turn away and say, "Forget about the culture. All I'm going to do is build my church. We're going to recruit more people. We're going to disciple them. We're going to forget about what's happening in the world around us. We're just going to get serious about building our churches." That's what people are saying. It is a new kind of separatist fundamentalism that is gripping Evangelicals, where churches are saying, "We're going to turn inward."

But it would be wrong for us to do this. So wrong! Do not succumb to that temptation! If you don't remember anything else I say, remember these three words: "Despair is sin."

Remember also that the Bible tells us that we are to take dominion. We are to be fruitful, increase in number, fill the earth, subdue it, rule over the fish of the earth. We are to take every thought captive in obedience to Christ. We are to be concerned with the entire creation for which God has given us stewardship and responsibility. We should be caring about everything in the world around us, not just filling our own souls for our own satisfaction. That's biblical.

What's more, just looking at it from a tactical and strategic standpoint as we approach the eve of the millennium, if we were to retreat today, it would be like an army on the field of battle about to achieve a great victory, and then turning away and retreating. I say that because I'm one of those who believes that Pope John Paul II is absolutely right when he says in "Redemptoris Missio" that the third millennium will be a "springtime for Christianity"—that it can be the greatest harvest of souls ever! That it can be the greatest opportunity ever!

We're already seeing signs of it. Teenage pregnancies are down in the last three years. Nobody can quite explain why. I think I know why. Not so much because of what we're preaching, but because modern man has reached the point where he has achieved his ultimate goal in life. The thing he wanted more than anything else was autonomy, "The right to do whatever I want to do." But autonomy leads you to the point where, once you get it, you can't live with the consequences. Autonomy creates chaos in a culture when everyone does what is right in his own eyes. It creates chaos. And now kids are being shot in school, families are breaking up, and people are looking around saying, "I don't like what's happening in my neighborhood." Polling this week showed that people said the number-one problem in America is declining morality.

They're waking up to the fact that getting what they want—personal autonomy—has created exactly the opposite of the way they want to live. Modern man has run out the string. He's gotten what he wanted, and he can't live with it. So we're seeing the beginnings of a change.

Besides teenage pregnancies being "down," abortions also have come down in the last five years. This is partly a result of people having a better understanding of abortion (because of the debate over the partial-birth abortion bill), but also because people's values are changing.

And the crime rate is coming down. Not because we're building more prisons, but because we're doing things differently in our communities and beginning to work with kids in a different way.

THE GOSPEL DOES INDEED TRANSFORM NOT ONLY THE HUMAN HEART, BUT ALSO THE SOCIETY IN WHICH WE LIVE.

And even the moral debate is shifting in America. A year ago when I went on television, if I made the statement that private immorality has public consequences, nobody would listen. But in the last month, I've been on *Hardball*, and I've been with Fred Barnes, and I've been on *Nightline* with Ted Koppell, and I've been on with Larry King, and the discussion on each program was about the question, "What is repentance? What's the right moral response?" And nobody today in America would say that private immorality does not have public consequences. The debate is shifting.

So for Christians at this particular point in time to back away, to stop engaging the culture, would be an act of biblical betrayal of massive proportions. It would be wrong. We mustn't do it. We must engage the culture.

Let me tell you what I've seen over the last twenty-five years: When Christians really set out to engage the culture, when Christians really set out to make a difference in the world around us, we see in the most dramatic and powerful ways that the gospel does indeed transform not only the human heart, but also the society in which we live.

I see it in a little microcosm in two prison units in South America that are run by Prison Fellowship; they're Christian prisons, and you sense the presence and power of God in those prisons. One is in San Jose dos Campos, Brazil; one is in Quito, Ecuador—the Garcia Moreno Prison. One wing of Garcia Moreno, the detainees' wing, is one of the worst prisons I have ever been in. There's blood on the doorsteps; there are garbage piles around the prison with dogs rummaging through it; torture cells that are still being used; twelve men in a cell with four bunks, and open sewage.

I was there with a group of corrections officials from the States. In the afternoon, four hundred men were milling in the courtyard, because they were all let out at the same time, only one hour a day. We'd traveled all this way, and then a guard told us in Spanish that we couldn't go in. Here I was, a former marine captain, bringing all these guys down here. . .nobody's going to tell me that I can't go in there! So I said to our Prison Fellowship director in Ecuador, "You tell him that we want to go in," knowing that he probably wasn't going to let us. I mean, I figured I was safe. . . . You never want to take a gamble like that, because the guard and the Prison Fellowship director started to argue in Spanish (I had no idea what they were saying), and the next thing I knew the guard said, *"Sí,"* and they opened the gate for us to go into that crowded prison yard. One of my assistants pushed me in and said, "Go preach the gospel," then he backed off. What had I done?

But it turned out to be one of the most amazing experiences! I walked into the center of that yard with one other man and just stood there. Very soon, all those men gathered around me. Most of them had been in prison five years and didn't know the charges against them; stumps of arms, eyes gouged out, and sores all over them; it was something out of a Dickens novel. I've never seen such depravity. The walls were lined with women, or so I thought—fully formed breasts, lipstick and all—but it turned out that they were transvestites. Smells were overpowering. It was the most awful place I'd ever been in my life. And yet I preached the gospel that day and saw how those men responded, many weeping in that yard.

Then we went a hundred yards out of that detainees' wing, into the San Pablo wing of the prison and walked through a set of huge doors. This is the wing that Prison Fellowship has taken over. We walked out of filth and slime and sewage and depravity, and through the doors into a church filled with three hundred men, some playing guitars, singing, praising the Lord, with an altar set up at the end of the cell block. That's the cell block run by Prison Fellowship. And when they saw us coming, these guys—perfect strangers—got up, came running over and threw their arms around us. Of course they weren't strangers at all; they were brothers. That whole place was transformed into a clean, orderly environment full of life.

Governor Bush, just elected in Texas, sent one of his assistants on the trip who reported this to him, and the governor gave us permission to open a Prison Fellowship prison unit in Texas. I was just there ten days ago, and it was one of the most memorable days of my ministry. It's called the InnerChange Freedom Initiative, and it's in the Jester II prison just outside of Houston. This is a prison unit in which we take the responsibility for the programming—all programming.

Anybody who's been in prison knows what horrid, hopeless, desperate places they are. But I walked in this Texas prison unit, and there was such joy. Some of the men in that place have given up parole, because it takes eighteen months to complete the program. We had a graduation ceremony for the first group which had completed the course. As they were coming through the line, there was one man, Ron Flowers, walking toward me to get his certificate. I looked out of the corner of my eye and saw a tall woman stand up and walk toward us. I knew who she was.

We have something called the Sycamore Tree Project, where inmates work with our counselors on issues of repentance and restitution. And this one inmate, Ron Flowers, had insisted upon his innocence throughout his fourteen years in prison. But one night in prayer, he said, "I've got to confess it. I did indeed murder the woman I was charged with murdering." Someone contacted the pastor of the mother of the woman who had been murdered. This mother and her pastor came to that prison. They spent four hours on their knees with the man who had killed her daughter. Many tears were shed that night. Finally the mother turned to Ron Flowers and said, "You took my daughter's life. You took my husband's life, because he died of a broken heart. But I'm a Christian, and I forgive you." The two embraced.

So when Ron Flowers walked across the stage for me to hand him his graduation certificate, this woman, Mrs. Washington, got up out of her chair and walked over and threw her arms around Ron and told the crowd she was now Ron Flowers' adopted mom. I looked out over the faces of two hundred convicts, every single one of them crying. That whole place was transformed by an act of supernatural grace, because Christians have gone into this prison culture and witnessed to the love of Christ and have seen God changing people's hearts; in doing so, He changes a prison culture. I don't know if I'd have the courage to do, or the faith to do, what I saw Mrs. Washington do. But that's the grace of God.

Again, what's happened in these prisons is a microcosm of the larger culture. It's a metaphor, a parable, for all of life. If we really go in and take the gospel and live it out in every aspect of life, we transform that culture! That can happen in America as Christians live out their faith, get out of their comfortable padded pews, and go out and do the gospel. Live it out in areas like that, and you change that culture.

I suggest that there are four things that we ought to be doing.

Knowing Two World Views

The first might be a bit of a shock. Christianity does not begin or end with John 3:16; it does not begin or end with your salvation. "I'm saved; you're saved; we're okay" is not the gospel. That's therapy. The gospel is a life system; biblical revelation is reality, ultimate reality. We see all of life through the prism of God's eyes. Everything!

When dedicating Free University, which he founded in Amsterdam, Abraham Kuyper, the great Dutch theologian and president of the Netherlands at the turn of the twentieth century, said, "There is not one square inch in the whole domain of human existence over which Christ who is sovereign does not cry out 'Mine'!" Music, science, sociology, politics—every single area of life is God's, and the job of a Christian with a biblical world view is to see the world through God's eyes, to recognize that God is not only the One who justified us through His Son, Jesus Christ, but also He is the One who spoke this universe into existence, the sovereign Creator God. The job of the Church is to take and bring that truth to bear on every area of life.

Which is why I so love the Gaither Praise Gathering. Not only are you lifting up music, which is inspirational and joyous to experience and be a part of in our fellowship together, but you are also creating something that penetrates the imagination of people, not just their minds, but touches them at the deepest level. And Christians have to do this in every single area of life. A biblically informed world view embraces the whole of life; it is a world view and a life system.

It's absolutely essential to understand our world view if we are to live a rational life. You've got to know the physical order and the moral order God has created. You've got to understand something of the law of gravity in order not to fall off a platform. Similarly, you've got to know the moral laws God has created in order to live just and fulfilled lives. Not to know what God has created is like walking into a dark room full of furniture and not turning on the lights.

EVERY SINGLE AREA OF LIFE IS GOD'S, AND THE JOB OF A CHRISTIAN WITH A BIBLICAL WORLD VIEW IS TO SEE THE WORLD THROUGH GOD'S EYES.

And you've got to understand a biblical view of life in order to evangelize well in today's world. If I walked into this crowd and said, "Jesus is the answer," you'd all know what I meant. You walk into a secular crowd and say, "Jesus is the answer," and they don't know there's a question! Their response is, "What's the question?" So you can say you're saved from your sins, but they don't believe they're sinners. Francis Schaeffer was right, there has to be cultural evangelism, preevangelism, and you've got to show people the fallacies of their way of thinking. And you've got to also understand the world view the secularist lives by in order to engage him and, of course, in order to transform that culture.

What's at stake today in the culture war is not a battle over homosexual rights; it is not a battle over abortion. Those are just the manifestations of the deeper cosmic struggle between two ways of understanding reality. The secular view says there's a naturalistic explanation for everything, the Christian view says no, there's a supernatural explanation. The secular world says this moment is all that matters; the Christian says no, eternity is what counts. The secular world says everything is subjective—what I think it is at the moment; the Christian says no, history matters because our God is a God of history. The Christian says there is an absolute physical and moral order and there is truth; the secular world says truth is whatever you find it to be, everything is relative; the Christian says no, there is truth. These are two great ways of understanding reality that are in conflict in the world today.

You can sum up the secular view very easily. I love philosophy. I've read it all my life, studied it in college, have Plato's *Republic* and Aristotle's *Politics* on my bookshelves in multivolumed editions. But we in modern America have taken philosophy and reduced it to a bumper sticker. Amazing! It's the McNugget generation; the *USA Today* format: Reduce everything to quick and easy. We've taken the philosophy of the ages and reduced it down to one word: whatever. A cartoon in the *Wall Street Journal* recently showed a minister marrying a couple. The groom is standing there with his hands in his pockets. He's kind of slouched over, and the minister says, "No, no, no. You're supposed to say, 'I do,' not 'whatever.' "

Then there's that dreadful bumper sticker that says, "If it feels good, do it." One of my good friends was following a car that had that sticker on its back bumper. The car came to a stoplight and stopped. My friend pulled up behind it, and he couldn't resist. BANG! He mildly hit the car's bumper. The driver's head spun around and he got out of the car. He asked, "What are you doing?" My friend said, "It felt good." The secular world is creating a way of life that says if it feels good, do it. But this bumper-sticker philosophy results in chaos. When people do what feels good, the whole society begins to crumble, and people discover they can't live with that.

If we understand the conflicting world views, we have a wonderful apologetic. If we stand up and say, "The Bible says you've got to do this," people aren't likely to hear us. But if we stand up and say, "Your system of thought leads you to ridiculous conclusions that you can't live with, and let me explain why," they listen. This brings me to my second point.

Articulating Two World Views

We have to be able to argue—present these cultural issues in terms the world can understand so we can win them over. I try to do this with my "BreakPoint" radio commentary every day. I did a commentary once on the Saab automobiles and their advertising line, "Find your own road." I said they weren't selling cars; they were selling the existentialist philosophy of the 1960s, which is do your own thing, live your own life. A week after the commentary, I got a call from the new president of Saab U.S. "Mr. Colson," he said, "I listened to your commentary. Then I studied our ads. You know, you're right. We're not selling cars; we're selling a philosophy. I'm pulling all those ads off the air." You see, if we can point out to people what they're doing and if we make sense, we can win the argument. The problem is they're blind; they don't see it. We have to help them.

And we have to do it lovingly. A friend, Ron Greer, an ex-offender and part-time pastor in Madison, Wisconsin, was presiding over his church one day when homosexual activists burst in and broke up the service. They were protesting the fact that Ron, who worked full-time in the fire department, was passing out tracts urging homosexuals to come to Christ and be changed. (He lost his job.) These homosexuals came into the church and hurled condoms onto the altar and screamed. But Ron didn't do anything; he just stood there. Afterward the press asked him, "Why didn't you react? Why didn't you get angry?" He said, "I had no more reason to get angry with them than if a blind man had stepped on my foot. They don't know any better." The world doesn't know any better! They have to see us as a loving community, loving them notwithstanding, but pointing out to them why their ways don't work.

My friend Robby George is a professor at Princeton, in his midforties and a devout Christian. Robby is one of the great political philosophers in America. He was invited to debate Stanley Fish. Stanley Fish is perhaps the leading deconstructionist in America. That means he believes all literature and history and law can be deconstructed, that it is not objectively true and is only a reflection of what people in power think. He is as far left on the spectrum academically and intellectually as you could imagine anybody to be. He goes around giving lectures, saying that there is no truth. He wrote a book, *There's No Such Thing As Free Speech and It's a Good Thing, Too!*

Robby George was scheduled to debate him before the American Society of Political Scientists on Labor Day weekend in Boston. Two hundred political scientists gathered from around the country. The issue was the pro-life verses pro-choice position. Robby George wrote a brief on pro-life. He never mentioned Scripture. He set out simply to prove that the baby in the womb is a human being, and he did it based on scientific and medical evidence. And he sent the brief ahead of time to Stanley Fish. Fish arrived at the meeting, stood up before that whole crowd, and said, "I have read Dr. George's brief carefully. I must confess that the pro-choice position is wrong, that life does begin in the womb; the evidence supporting the pro-life position is correct. I have been wrong."

It can be done!

Being Agents of Common Grace

Third, we've got to be agents of common grace. This is something we don't hear about often enough. John Calvin made a wonderful distinction between saving grace—that is, when God reaches down and converts you—and common grace. Saving grace—that's what I received twenty-five years ago in a friend's driveway when God transformed me; He regenerated me. I became a new person, a new creation in Christ. That's what saving grace is. But there's also common grace that God sheds abroad in His creation to hold back the flood of sin and chaos that would otherwise overwhelm us. And we're all to be instruments of common grace. So when we go into prisons, for example, we're bringing the love of Christ to bring men and women to Christ, but also to reduce the sin and injustice of that prison, and in this effort we are instruments of common grace.

And there's so many ways we can do that! About eight years ago, I was at a prayer breakfast being held in conjunction with the National Association of Broadcasters convention where I was to speak. I was sitting next to this nice young woman, a Christian, from Hollywood. She was telling me how she thought it was her call to go to Hollywood, because she wanted to produce a Christian script and get it on prime-time evening TV. I listened to her. She was so idealistic, so full of enthusiasm and excitement that I didn't have the heart to tell her that she didn't have a prayer. She said, "I'm going to do it. I'm going to stay there until I do it." I said, "Well, I certainly wish you well." As I left, we had a little prayer together. Little faith that I had! That was Martha Williamson who created *Touched by an Angel*. It is broadcast all over America, indeed the world. Her program is a powerful instrument of common grace to its viewers.

We are agents of common grace when we go into the families' homes of those inmates, with Prison Fellowship Angel Tree. We reached nearly half a million kids across America last year. It's the greatest thing my wife, Patty, and I do every Christmas. Our grand-kids get lots of gifts. They open them up. After five minutes, they put them back under the tree or throw them somewhere. But you go into those homes where kids have nothing for Christmas, and Mommy or Daddy's locked up in prison. You say, "This is from your father who's in prison, and it's from your Father who's in heaven." And you read to them the birth of Jesus out of Luke. You give them some gospel literature. You offer to come back, because more and more, Angel Tree is turning into a year-round program. I see those little guys look up at me and say, "Oh, I knew my daddy wouldn't forget me!" There's nothing at Christmas we enjoy doing more.

WE'VE GOT TO STAND TOGETHER AS "MERE CHRISTIANS" IN THE NEW MILLENNIUM AND SAY WE LOVE GOD TOGETHER, SAY WE'RE GOING TO STAND TOGETHER AS THE CHURCH.

These children of prisoners are the kids growing up "at risk" of being the next wave of criminals. Don't tell me about new government programs for juveniles. The way to deal with the youth crime crisis is for Christians to go out and touch these kids with the love of God and take an interest in them, and one by one see God transform them. This would do more to reduce juvenile crime than all the government programs imaginable.

And that's being an instrument of common grace. And you can

do it in every walk of life. I've given you only a few brief illustrations.

Being Mere Christians

Fourth and finally, I know this point goes down hard sometimes with some folks, but it's something about which the Holy Spirit has deeply convicted me: As we approach the new millennium, we've got to do what C. S. Lewis says, we've got to be "mere Christians."

I gave the closing lecture at Cambridge on the one hundredth anniversary of Lewis's birth. It was a wonderful experience—two weeks of great music, poetry, artists. What I realized as we discussed Lewis was that he didn't come out of the Evangelical subculture, so he wasn't conditioned by all of our prejudices and beliefs. I held up his famous book, *Mere Christianity*, and asked the crowd if they realized why Lewis gave it the title he did. Lewis was saying, "The imperative thing is that Christians be 'mere' Christians," that is, that we not add hyphens or other qualifiers; we are first and foremost Christians— and we're Christians together.

Yes, we Christians among ourselves have doctrinal differences, long-standing ones that go back hundreds of years. And we've been negotiating and discussing, and we've been trying to find common ground to narrow these differences. But we're always going to have them. And we don't want to compromise truth. But the imperative thing as we approach the new millennium—if we really want to present to the world a loving community that draws people in—is that we must not be constantly fighting among ourselves. We've got to stand together as "mere Christians" in the new millennium and say we love God together, say we're going to stand together as the church.

"That they all may be one, as You, Father, are in Me, and I in You; that they also may be one in Us, that the world may believe that You sent Me." (John 17:21 NKJV). Orthodox, Catholic, Baptist, Presbyterian—He's calling us all not to compromise truth, but to be one with and part of a loving body—over 1,700,000,000 Christians around the world! If the world could see the love that I experience in a community inside the prisons, across denominational lines, they would be beating our doors down to come in.

The new millennium is going to be, I believe, a great springtime of hope. When John Paul II called the new millennium the "springtime for Christianity," I wondered if he was getting delusions in his old age. Old people often get sour, thinking that the younger generation can't do it as well as they did. They look askance at what's going on. But here's a seventy-eight-year-old man saying, no, the millennium is going to be the springtime of Christian harvest. Christians celebrate! The new millennium is going to be a wonderful period.

I had a real insight this summer as I began to finish the book I'm writing, *How Now Shall We Live?* We need to take a little longer view than last week's elections. Take a little longer view than the court case last summer. We need to see the broad sweep of history. Just look at this past century. It began with the post-Edwardian triumphalism at the early part of the century, best captured in the film *Titanic*. (My Baptist pastor says Christians shouldn't see that film because it has a nude scene in it. Just to be clear about this, I saw it on an airplane crossing the Atlantic, and it was an edited version.) There's an extraordinary moment in the beginning of the film when a passenger is about to get aboard this huge vessel. He's dressed in all of his finery to go into the first-class compartment. He looks at that ship and says, "There is a ship that even God couldn't sink." Never finished the first voyage. What arrogance. What a mockery of God.

The triumphalism of the early part of the century—the belief in science and the belief that man had all the answers—collapsed. Then we had the Hegelian influence arguing that man was going to get smarter and smarter; in doing so, we'd erase sin. It didn't happen. All the great utopian dreams of the twentieth century—failed. All the "-isms"—communism, national socialism, humanism have all proven bankrupt.

Why should we be engaging the culture? Because this is an extraordinary moment and opportunity, as we can look at a world disillusioned by all of the failed utopianisms of the twentieth century and say, "There still endures biblical revelation that gives a basis to order our lives rationally and sensibly and live together in peace and harmony. There's still the gospel of Jesus Christ—unchanged: 'Jesus Christ, the same yesterday, today, and forever,' who offers us salvation. We can't find redemption in this world any other way."

And as the world sees the shattered illusions of the twentieth century all crashing down upon them, they can still see that Cross at Calvary—still see that enduring truth of history. This indeed is a great moment for Christians! Don't turn away.

God bless you.

The Cultivation of Conscience

Wheaton College
Wheaton, Illinois
Commencement, 2000

My theme today is conscience—an appropriate one, I suggest, for graduates, as you go forth to serve Christ in your respective callings. Whatever your vocation, each of you will play a crucial role in forming the consciences of the people you serve, and through them, of society as a whole.

This is a more difficult task today than ever before in American history, or indeed Western history, because we are witnessing in our culture the near-death of conscience.

Conscience 101

At one level, we have God's word for it that conscience cannot be eradicated completely. We know this from Paul's discussion of law in Romans 2. There Paul uses the word *law* first in the sense that would be most familiar to his audience, largely Jewish converts living in Rome. There are, Paul says, those "under" the revealed law and those who are "without," or outside of, the law. But then he shifts to another sense of "law," a universal sense of the "work of the law" that human beings know just by virtue of their humanity. Only Jews know the "law" in the first sense, but everyone knows it in the latter sense. Paul writes:

> *For when Gentiles who do not have the Law do instinctively* [other translations say, "by nature"] *the things of the Law, these, not having the Law, are a law to themselves, in that they show the work of the Law written in their hearts, their conscience bearing witness, and their thoughts alternately accusing or else defending them.*
> ROMANS 2:14–15, NASB

All people have a conscience sensitive to the law of God by virtue of their having been created in His image and likeness.

But there are signs that this God-given internal moral compass may be faltering in this generation. I confront this brutal truth regularly in prisons across this country. I remember one incident in Indiana a few years ago, which brought it home to me dramatically. This was a prison I had visited several times before. But this day a young inmate responded to my proffered handshake by smacking my hand away. This was a first for me. In years of visiting prisons, I had never before encountered such direct and immediate hostility. I saw it in the eyes of so many, particularly younger, men. Prisoners are almost never cheerful, but that day I saw in those eyes a depth of chill and lifelessness that I had not seen before.

The assistant warden was a Christian whom I had known for years, so I asked him what was happening. "This place has changed," I added.

"Changed?" he asked. "Indeed it has. Ten years ago I could talk to these kids about right and wrong. Now they don't know what I'm talking about." He went on to say that the older prisoners were demanding protection from the newly arrived nineteen- or twenty-year-olds. This was an ominous reversal: Historically in corrections, the younger guys needed protection from the older cons.

Paul wasn't wrong. People are still born with that spark of natural awareness of right and wrong. But we must remember that that spark needs to be kindled, the conscience has to be cultivated, or it will begin to harden.

Cultivated Conscience

Conscience is cultivated primarily within the God-ordained structures of family and church. But when families break down and churches fail in their duties, it stands to reason that children will grow up with severely underformed, even malformed, consciences. And we know the social consequences. Profs. James Wilson and Richard Herrnstein, in their landmark 1985 study "Crime and Human Nature," found the chief cause of crime to be the lack of moral training during the morally formative years.

THE CONSCIENCE HAS TO BE CULTIVATED, OR IT WILL BEGIN TO HARDEN.

The horrifying truth is that we have bred a generation of kids with unformed consciences. They are like feral children raised in the wilderness, and they have unleashed a wave of terror in our streets and our schools.

Besides the family and church, the man-made institution of the school should play its role in the formation of conscience. But there is little help in today's schools. In fact, the "values" instruction pervasive in our schools often does more harm than good. Prof. Sidney Simon's much-celebrated "values clarification" curriculum and its variations confront children with morally anguishing choices. Such choices can indeed occur in life, and there is nothing inherently wrong with discussing them in the classroom—provided that a solid foundation of basic morality has been laid. And this is precisely what such courses do not do. Instead, they give children morally difficult hypotheticals, with no resources to fall back on except what the child "feels" would be the right thing to do—or what works or what leads to the best results (with no yardstick for defining "best").

Unfortunately, what some of our children believe "feels right" or "works" is truly terrifying. Eric Harris and Dylan Klebold "clarified" their "values" quite thoroughly: their hate, their rage, and their self-obsession. Just look at the extraordinary tapes they made before they began their mad rampage in Littleton.

Corrupted Conscience

Of course this identification of conscience with "what feels right" does not come solely from "values clarification" courses. It is part of the everyday moral language of our society. Robert Bellah first chronicled it in *Habits of the Heart:* Americans, he found, know of no higher or more reliable basis for morality than their feelings. James Davison Hunter found the same thing in researching his book on the culture wars, titled *Before the Shooting Begins.*

It's just as philosopher Alasdair MacIntyre said: The end result of Nietzsche's deconstruction of morality was not a race of over-men "saying yes to life" in a world beyond good and evil, but a world of people clinging to a thin notion of right and wrong that rests on a purely emotional basis, not a rational or empirical one. The buzz-words of this new mode of moral thinking are "it feels right" or "it works for me."

In the sixteenth, seventeenth, and eighteenth centuries, philosophers argued over whether knowledge, including moral knowledge, is "rational" (that is, known to the mind intuitively) or "empirical" (that is, based on experience or experimentation). But today both these bases are rejected, and pure passion is substituted in their place. The rationalists and the empiricists at least agreed that there is a moral order to be discerned; modern subjectivism rejects even this assumption, except insofar as that order lies within the individual and passionately felt will.

It's bad enough that we have failed to train the consciences of the young. Even more insidious, we have corrupted conscience for all of us, deconstructing its very definition. The most visible example of this, unhappily, is found in the highest office in our nation. During the sordid disclosures in the Monica Lewinsky scandal, President Clinton repeatedly stared at the cameras, telling the nation that his conscience was clear, that he was at peace with himself about his own behavior; all the while he knew exactly what he had done. But he was, I believe, utterly sincere; for as later interviews and disclosures made clear, what he meant was that he did not feel that the kind of sex he engaged in was wrong, and since it wasn't, he felt lying was not wrong. This is the quintessential expression of a conscience totally subjectivized by the value system of the 1960s: It feels right, so it must be right.

Just because I am a political conservative who once worked in a Republican White House, don't conclude that I see President Clinton as in any way unique—excessive perhaps—but not unique. On the contrary, he is everyman or, perhaps more precisely, every man in power. We certainly betrayed our consciences in Watergate. I learned that people under stress have an infinite capacity for self-rationalization. And, as I discovered in my own life, we're never more dangerous than when we're self-righteous about it. If anything is different today, it is that the subjective process—the substitution of feelings for objective reality—has intensified.

This way of thinking—whether it's used by White House officials hiding evidence, or people betraying their spouses, or kids about to shoot their classmates—reflects a corruption of the very nature of conscience. Consider what Cardinal John Henry Newman, the nineteenth-century English Catholic churchman, wrote about conscience in the course of a dispute about the loyalty of English Catholic subjects. In his letter to the duke of Norfolk, Newman wrote:

> *Conscience has rights because it has duties; but in this age, with a large portion of the public, it is the very right and freedom of conscience to dispense with conscience. . . . Conscience is a stern monitor, but in this century it has been superseded by a counterfeit, which the eighteen centuries prior to it never heard of, and could not have mistaken for it, if they had. It is the right of self-will.*
>
> *That's the core of the problem. We've transformed the concept of conscience into self-will.*

Conscience 201

Traditionally, conscience was a form of knowledge. The very word *conscience* is made up of the Latin prefix *con*, meaning "with," followed by the word *science*, which comes from the word *scire*, "to know." Conscience was not direct, empirical knowledge, but a sort of knowledge that comes alongside empirical knowledge—"with-knowledge," if you will.

Because this "with-knowledge" is not empirical, perhaps it is what the philosophers call "analytic," that is, made up of propositions that cannot not be true. This may be a reach, but at least it links the idea of conscience with what Paul says in Romans 2 about man's natural knowledge of the law: It's "written on the heart." In the wonderful words of the very able natural-law theorist J. Budziszewski, it is that law that "we cannot not know."

"CONSCIENCE IS NOT THE POWER TO DETERMINE WHAT IS GOOD BUT TO RECOGNIZE WHAT IS GOOD AND TO CHOOSE ACCORDINGLY."

JOHN M. HAAS

Or, as moral theologian John M. Haas puts it: "Conscience is not the power to determine what is good but to recognize what is good and to choose accordingly."

Understood this way, it is not surprising that conscience was what held up the stop sign when our self-will was going full tilt. How different things are today. Now we give the name "conscience" to that self-loving instinct that shouts "go for it" whenever we're about to do something cruel or merely selfish.

As Princeton Prof. Robert P. George puts it:

> Consider how common it is for people to reason as follows: "My conscience does not tell me that X is wrong; therefore X is not wrong for me." Or, even more egregiously: "My conscience does not tell me that X is wrong (or wrong for me); therefore I have a right to do X as a matter of freedom of conscience. Every manner of evil and injustice is today rationalized, defended, and insulated from rebuke by appeal to conscience.

As Professor George points out, it's an easy step from turning conscience into a reliable green light for whatever course of conduct feels most desirable or expedient—which is quite bad enough—to claiming an actual right to engage in that conduct. And if it's a right, why not claim it's a constitutional right? And if it's a constitutional right, why not claim a legal immunity even from criticism by others? And so to protect a woman's constitutional "right" to kill her unborn child, we get laws like the Freedom of Access to Clinic Entrances Act that impose restrictions on the rights of opponents of abortion to even challenge that "right"—restrictions that would not be tolerated for any other reason.

Indeed this new doctrine of conscience has been raised to the level of constitutional law by the Supreme Court in its dreadful 1992 abortion decision, *Planned Parenthood v. Casey.* In this decision the Court announced that, even though *Roe v. Wade* may have been an act of judicial overreaching, and even though there are some good arguments against abortion, abortion must nonetheless remain a constitutional right—why? Because the Supreme Court said that "at the heart of liberty is the right to define one's own concepts of existence, of meaning, of the universe, and of the mystery of human life."

Newman would recognize this. It's the concept of self-will, unheard of until the nineteenth century, yet now declared to be a constitutional right!

Thus it is that we no longer think of conscience as an inner moral compass calibrated to true north; it is rather like a Ouija board that points in the direction we choose. In which event, the familiar expression "let your conscience be your guide," which might in an earlier time have been a reasonable adage, is now the most dangerous thing we can say to someone. It is an invitation to do wrong and feel good about it.

I would like to be able to tell you that the churches in this country are mounting some resistance and calling people back to an understanding of conscience as the "with-knowing" monitor of conduct that it used to be. Unfortunately, many churches have embraced the culture of subjective experience and feeling. In some cases, this has come about as a consequence of churches marketing themselves to an increasingly consumerist public, which seeks warm, personal experiences (and so we get "seeker-driven" churches, and the like). In other cases, it arises out of an unbalanced emphasis on the experiential side of the Christian's faith-walk. Either way, the churches are showing evidence of a critical and damaging shift in their view of God: God has ceased to be the *Bonum in se,* the Good in Himself, and has become merely the *Bonum mihi,* the good for me. Thus, the church is unable to be what it should be: the ultimate bulwark against subjectivism, emotivism, and the corruption of conscience.

Theologian and social critic Michael Novak, in a 1994 speech entitled "The Causes of Virtue," put his finger precisely on the public consequences determined by the state of individual consciences. "This country ought to have, when it is healthy and when it is working as it was intended to work, 250 million policemen called consciences. When there are 250 million consciences on guard, it is surprising how few police are needed on the streets."

But the converse is equally true. The fewer consciences on guard, the more police required. People are restrained only by the inner check of conscience or by the outer check of the sword. So if conscience is crippled, the sword must do the whole job. And the more the sword is required, the less freedom we enjoy. This is why the death of conscience eventually leads to tyranny.

Reviving Family, Church, and Academy

What, then, shall we as Christians do?

We must work to renew and revive the fundamental conscience-forming institutions of society—especially the family and church. Each of you will have many opportunities to influence the direction and shape of each of these important institutions as you leave Wheaton College and embark on your callings.

The family is absolutely fundamental, and yet it is in danger of being destroyed through redefinition. If everything is a family, then nothing is a family, and that, I suspect, is the result desired by those pressing to redefine the family. There are many reasons why the survival of the family is essential to society, chief among them its crucial role in developing the conscience. Whatever our calling, all of us must work to strengthen the biblical model of the family and to defend the institution in the public square.

THE FAMILY IS ABSOLUTELY FUNDAMENTAL, AND YET IT IS IN DANGER OF BEING DESTROYED THROUGH REDEFINITION.

In addition, the church has a role to play in cultivating individual and corporate conscience. A letter written by an early Christian to a pagan friend said that Christians in society are like the soul in the body. We must get past the feel-good model of church building and strive to build authentic communities of faith, in which conscience as the "stern but wise monitor" is nurtured, in which strong, serious disciples serve one another by holding one another to the objective standards of biblical righteousness. And churches can do what no other institution in society can do today, which is to teach ethics. By doing these things, we help build a crucial firewall against the corruption of conscience through subjectivism and emotivism.

Which leads me to the charge that I want to leave with you this day.

I would ask you first to consider the challenge faced by Wheaton College and the Christian academy in general. Many of you will leave Wheaton with fond memories. You'll return for reunions and the like. But more is required of you. I hope that as beneficiaries of one of the best educations available anywhere, as graduates of a school that has a great leadership responsibility in the Christian world, you will continue to see yourself as part of the Wheaton community of scholars, that you will care deeply about and encourage Wheaton, especially in its commitment to moral education and the cultivation of conscience. For this is today one of the most crucial responsibilities of the Christian academy, a responsibility it largely carries alone.

Though the secular academy, often reflecting its religious roots, historically maintained a commitment to moral education, it has today sadly almost totally abandoned it. This is a rather recent development. As late as 1870, it caused a big dust-up at Yale when William Graham Sumner chose to use a book by Herbert Spencer in an upper-level sociology course. Spencer was a Darwinist, and Yale President Noah Porter was alarmed that his students were being taught a world view without a Creator. Until the middle of the nineteenth century, Christian ethics were taught to Harvard undergraduates by the president himself. And as recently as the mid-1950s (at least that seems recent to me), when I was an undergraduate, chapel was mandatory at my alma mater, Brown University, which has today become a hotbed of politically correct liberalism.

Where the modern retreat from moral commitment leads was evident in a letter to alumni from Gordon Gee, the recently resigned president of Brown University. Gee writes:

> *I believe that we should discuss values at this university*
> *and that our students should be free to choose to study them*
> *intently and to discuss them publicly. This does not mean that*

Brown will endorse or teach a specific value system. It does mean that we intend to make Brown a place where values are discussed in depth and often, where ideas are challenged both by the institution and by individuals—always with civility, respect, and community spirit.

So Brown has no convictions whatsoever about right conduct—only a commitment to a discussion about subjective feelings. One has to wonder how the values of "civility, respect, and community spirit" will be agreed upon. But of course there's the rub. In the end the only moral values can be whatever those convening the discussion say they are. In postmodernism there is only one ultimate certainty: power.

Wheaton and schools like it stand alone, as institutions that still believe in absolutes and can therefore provide moral education. Indeed we have a sacred trust to do this. I thank God for Wheaton and institutions like it, where the Bible is at the heart of what we believe and affects how we see every discipline and how we structure campus life.

But I would suggest that even Wheaton might ask itself on a regular basis how consistently it makes moral education a priority in curriculum and campus life. For Wheaton and other Christian institutions face an entirely different challenge today than they did even a generation ago. One can no longer assume that students coming to this institution have had the benefit of the moral formation that ideally comes from families and schools. The corruption of conscience of which I have spoken is so pervasive that I suspect it has unconsciously affected many Christian families. I know it has affected the church. And it stands to reason that Christian young people are buffeted by the nihilism and degradation of popular culture to nearly as great a degree as their secular counterparts.

I am sure you realize also that students are arriving on campus from high schools in which moral education has been thoroughly relativized. Even in the case of students from what we used to call "good families"—meaning intact families with parents who loved, guided, and encouraged their children—very different influences will have had twelve school years to whittle away the consciences they were born with and which their families nurtured.

THERE IS SUCH A THING AS TRUTH. . .AND IT IS THE HIGHEST SCHOLARLY PURSUIT TO SEEK IT.

Because of influences like this, moral education must be woven into every aspect of the educational experience. This means that students straight off need to be disabused of the notion that there are no absolutes, no objective standards of right and wrong, and that if one asserts that there are, he has committed an offense against our tolerant society and exposed himself as a Bible-thumping, know-nothing or worse. This is in the first instance, of course, an epistemological task. Students need to be taught that there is such a thing as truth: that which conforms to reality, that which reflects the way things really are; and it is the highest scholarly pursuit to seek it.

Christians have an advantage here, because God's revelation has given us a framework for knowing truth. We understand there is a physical order. We see the evidence of it in intelligent design, and we know it to be the handiwork of a Creator God. We understand as well that if God has created the physical order, God has also created a moral order, the character of which He has also made known to us.

There is truth and it is knowable. And for the Christian, this reality, as I have argued in my new book *How Now Shall We Live?*, forms a world view that is rationally sustainable and livable as no other world view is. Students—and for that matter all of us—need to be firmly grounded in our world view, that is, a comprehensive framework for understanding how the world works, for answering the questions of where we came from, why there is sin and suffering, and how we can be redeemed from it. This world view informs our understanding of all of life.

And it is this world view that enables us to apprehend the objective standards of right and wrong, which necessarily flow from it. Thus it is that with such a world view we can in the Christian academy teach ethics, which secular institutions have lost the capacity to do. What's more, we are able to draw certain parameters for our behavior, which is to say—rules.

This is an appropriate task for a college. The very word *college,* if you unpack it, turns out to mean "law-together." Originally it was a group of scholars who had their privileges and immunities vis-à-vis the municipal and national authorities and who governed themselves in their pursuit of learning. Being a self-governing body necessarily entails rules: not just individual standards, but standards applied at the group level. A Christian college has to make and enforce rules—in the most obvious instance, against academic dishonesty.

But it will also need to make rules regarding personal lifestyle. I know Wheaton already does this, so I'm not preaching to this choir, but rather suggesting a challenge for Christian colleges and other institutions generally. Admittedly, there is a risk to a college's public image: In this day and age, who wants to be thought prudish or repressive? But if a Christian college is really a group of Christian scholars who are bound by "law-together," they have to set Christian standards.

If it sounds tough to set rules on what students have been conditioned to think of as purely "private" conduct, think about the knots that colleges get tied up in over issues of sexual harassment and the like. All over the country students and faculty are being investigated, and even expelled, or fired over sexual conduct—the very thing that colleges seemed, back in the seventies, to have abandoned totally to a regime of anarchy, or of purely individualistic rule-making. The U.S. Supreme Court even has on its docket this year a case that arose out of a collegiate sexual encounter. We threw sexual morality out the front door in the sixties only to have it return through the back door in the nineties, via the civil rights laws. In the sixties men got laughed at if they behaved chivalrously. Today they get sued if they don't—although they still can't call it chivalry.

In speaking about rules, we should be clear that rules must genuinely serve the spiritual good. Rules enforced by some Christian colleges have been much in the news recently, but these are rules in my opinion with no scriptural foundation. Obviously, we should ensure that any set of rules is well grounded, not mere human preference.

I realize this is a controversial subject, and I will readily acknowledge that rules per se will not ensure the sanctification of students or anyone else. But rules—whether they guide our personal lives, our family relations, or our professional conduct—act as a moral teacher. They communicate the conviction of the community that there are some absolute standards of right and wrong—some things we all understand we ought to do, some things we ought not to do.

The effort to live by them can be a crucial exercise in developing discipline. When I was in the U.S. Marine Corps the rules rigidly imposed upon us were given a particular name by marines, which I could not repeat on a Christian campus. Yet living by the rules taught me invaluable lessons in personal discipline, lessons that have stuck with me all of my life. (The rules at the time seemed arbitrary and capricious, but in hindsight I've come to appreciate their wisdom.) Human beings need guidelines and guardrails.

Virtuous Lives of Gratitude

But there is more we must attend to, which applies not only to the Christian academy but to all of us, whatever our calling. For one thing, we need to learn, and encourage others to learn, the classic virtues and to study the lives of great men and women who have exemplified those virtues. Heroes fulfill an important role. My friend Bill Bennett has shown us that people often learn more from moral literature than from moral philosophy.

And you need to be certain that you and your ministry—and those you teach, if you're in education—are well grounded in history. G. K. Chesterton called gratitude "the mother of all virtues." But if we do not understand our history, we have no sense of debt to those who went before us and often through great sacrifice paved the way for us.

> GRATITUDE FOR WHAT CHRIST HAS DONE FOR US AT THE CROSS IS WHAT MOTIVATES THE CHRISTIAN TO A LIFE OF OBEDIENCE AND RIGHTEOUSNESS.

We in this country and in the West in general owe an enormous debt to those who made possible the political freedoms and cultural heritage we enjoy today. When we realize this, we are then compelled to live lives worthy of that trust.

This truth was driven home powerfully in the magnificent film *Saving Private Ryan*. In the closing scene, Captain Miller, played by Tom Hanks, is slumped, bleeding profusely, against a tank. As he is losing consciousness, he stares at Private Ryan, whose life he has saved, and breathes out his last words: "Earn it." Ryan's young anguished face then morphs into the face of Ryan now fifty years later, who is on his hands and knees speaking to Miller's grave marker at Normandy. "I have lived my life as best I could. I hope I've earned what you have done for me," he pleads. Then with tears rolling down his cheeks, he turns to embrace his wife: "Tell me I've been a good man." Gratitude, you see, activates the stern monitor of conscience. And gratitude for what Christ has done for us at the Cross is what motivates the Christian to a life of obedience and righteousness. It is what keeps the conscience pointed to true north.

Transcendent View of Reality

This brings me to a final point. While we live in a world that exalts the momentary, we who are Christians must be distinctly countercultural. Students, indeed all Christians, need a transcendent view of reality. We should deal with today's problems with the ever-present realization that the things of this world will pass away and with the picture in our minds of Christ on His throne judging all.

This is a great moment for Christian education, for the church, and for each of you who will take away degrees today and embark upon your appointed callings. For the polls tell us that Americans are increasingly restless, dissatisfied with the moral nihilism so widespread in our culture. Increasing numbers of Americans are discovering that what they were promised, the *summa bonum* of life—personal autonomy—not only fails to satisfy their deepest needs but has left them alone, rootless, afraid to send their kids to school. Americans can't quite articulate it yet, but they are seeking a better way to order their lives.

But who will offer it? Who can point the way to a renewal of individual conscience and in turn the renewal of decency and righteousness in our society? Where will leaders of honor and virtue come from?

The non-Christian family is in a shambles. Public schools and the secular academy, mired in philosophical relativism, lack the capacity to teach even basic ethics, let alone inspire men and women to the heroic exertion necessary for the moral renewal of a culture.

This then is the great opportunity for those who go forth from the Christian academy as servants of the Lord in society. We are uniquely equipped to be and to raise up men and women passionately committed to living for God in the light of His truth in every field, passionately committed to the development of personal character and the renewal of conscience as the stern monitor of objective truth.

God bless you as you live your lives worthy of the trust placed in you.

The Christian Mind in the New Millennium

Wilberforce Conference
Colorado Springs, Colorado
October, 1999

I have the task here of distilling what took two and a half years of work on Nancy Pearcey's part and my part, and we were also helped by many scholars who read manuscripts and helped us with ideas—a tremendously collaborative effort, entitled *How Now Shall We Live?* The book is basically about a Christian world view, and I start by defining what we mean by that.

World view. You have heard that term thrown around so many times, how can I get it down in a few distinct words? I can talk about it reflecting ultimate reality. I can talk about it being the understanding of truth, which, of course, it is. But in plain old-fashioned common terms, it is trying to understand how the world works and how we fit into it.

Everybody goes through life developing a world view of some sort. You try to figure out what makes things work the way they do and how you fit into it all. You follow three basic questions that philosophers typically have asked from the beginning of time: (1) Where did I come from, and who are we? (2) Why is there this mess in which I am living? As Tolstoy put it, "Why do I know what is right and do what is wrong?" How do I cope with the human dilemma? (3) Is there an answer for me? Is there a meaning? Is there purpose for life? Start asking those questions, and answers come to you from all quarters. And your job in life is to sort out what is true and what is not true.

Here we are quickly going to look at the contours of a Christian world view, compare it briefly with other world views (we have done this more extensively in the book), and see what is true.

Needing a True Map
What is true?

Let's think in terms of a road map. You say, "I want to start in Detroit and end up in Huntington, West Virginia." You could put it into your computer or call AAA and say, "Give me a map." They send you that map, and you leave your home in Detroit and head off to Huntington, West Virginia, but you end up instead in Cincinnati, Ohio. You would say that that road map wasn't very reliable. And so you get another one. This time you end up in Chicago, and you say that that road map wasn't very reliable. Finally, you get a road map, and it takes you to Huntington, West Virginia. That road map was true. It conformed to reality, the way things really are.

The greatest pursuit in life is to try to find out the way things really are. What is true? What conforms to reality? What is it that makes the world around me work the way it works? And how do I find my place in it? In answering these questions, we use that term *world view*. You might think it is an academic term used only by professors who sit around in ivy-covered buildings, smoking pipes, wearing tweed jackets, and talking about world views. It isn't. It is a very understandable, common practical matter. For all of us are living out a world view all of the time.

And you must see that Christianity is a world view; it is more than simply salvation, although it will never be less than that. I, for one, will never forget the moment that Christ came into my life. I still feel deep, powerful emotions that I felt that night, as if it were yesterday. But Christianity is more than that, in the sense that it is ultimate reality, a road map for all of life and for every single aspect of life. The task we have is to understand that road map and then use it as a foundation to develop our lives, our disciplines, and our talents in such a way that we are following that road map and carrying out what God has called us to do in the world, to the end that ultimately we reform—just as William Wilberforce did—the culture of our day, either by renewing the culture or by building a new culture.

THE GREATEST PURSUIT IN LIFE IS TO TRY TO FIND OUT THE WAY THINGS REALLY ARE.

Battle of Belief Systems

The word *culture* comes from the word *cult,* which is a belief system. At the root of any culture is a belief system. Ideas have consequences, as Richard Weaver so famously said. Abraham Kuyper, the great Dutch theologian, who at one time was prime minister of his country, spoke of a battle in the world—a battle of first principles. (The battle is the same today as it was in his time a century ago.) It is a battle of two great world views, a cosmic struggle for the hearts and minds of people. We are at ground zero. We are right in the midst of that battle in this country today. Let me explain why.

Unless we see that it is a battle of world views, we will miss what is going on. I was talking with Senator Brownback about the confusion over the Kansas Board of Education's decision, where Christians are portrayed in the media as these "backward, religious bigots wanting to suppress the teaching of science in the classroom." Utter nonsense! Yet you saw all the columnists whipped into a lather over what they call "academic freedom"—that Christians are trying to suppress academic freedom. That is a precise reverse of what was really happening. It wasn't the Christians trying to suppress academic freedom. The Christians were saying that if you are going to teach evolution, fine. Simply teach all the evidence about evolution; just teach all of it. Teach the things about evolution that don't square with the evolutionary theory as well as the things that do.

Everybody was missing that it wasn't a battle over faith versus science or a battle over academic freedom; it was a battle over the fundamental building blocks of two distinct world views, because all world views flow out of the answer to the question, "Where did we come from?" Creation is the building block. So if you are dealing with the question of origins of the universe and of human beings, you are dealing with the fundamental building block of two conflicting world views.

Unless you understand that, you are always going to be fighting on the wrong ground. You are always going to be like a woman in Patty's Bible study who reported one day, "Oh, I'm so upset because my son in school was asked the origins of the universe. He wrote down 'God.' The teacher scratched it out, took twenty points off the exam, and said, 'No, it is the big bang!' " Everybody in the Bible study said, "Get a hold of Genesis and go running into that classroom and explain to that teacher what the Bible says."

When Patty came home and told me that (I was in the middle of writing something), I said, "Oh, no. Get that woman on the telephone, and let me explain to her what to do."

Don't go in and fight over faith versus science, because it isn't a question of faith versus science; it is a question of science. Ask where the big bang came from. Talk about the second law of thermodynamics. Talk about scientific questions, because the scientific is fast piling up on our side.

We've got to learn that at the root of most of the great struggles today is a clash of conflicting world views about questions of ultimate reality—how the world is organized, and how we fit into it. If Christians don't understand that, we are constantly going to be outgunned. Let me tell you, the other side understands. William Provine, a confirmed naturalist and professor at Cornell, got it absolutely right. He said, "If evolution is true, then there is no such thing as life after death. There is no ultimate foundation for ethics. There is no ultimate meaning for life. There is no free will." Of course! All of those things flow from your basic, fundamental answer to that question, "Where did we come from?"

The battle used to be among cultures in the world, among, say, the Islamic, Eastern mystical, African, and the Western Judeo-Christian traditions. And then, of course, there was the rise of the Enlightenment in the West. Those used to be the frontiers of world views in battle, in struggle. I don't think they are today. The struggle today is right here between two world views that are being battled out. We call it the culture war, but it is far more than that. It is battled out right here in our own society.

And because of the information and technological boom, it is traveling with lightning speed around the world, so that people in Africa are dealing with the same questions we are here. It is no longer a question of an Islamic and Eastern culture and tradition over there and the West over here—divisions along great religious and historical frontiers. It is the battle between secular naturalism and biblical theism. Every one of the struggles we see is being fought right here, and they are being transmitted instantly by the Internet.

Michael Cassedy, a great servant of Christ in South Africa, came to me and said, "I want to study with you, because I have been reading your materials, and we read the 'BreakPoint' commentaries." They get "BreakPoint" on the Internet in Africa! I said, "What relevance would our battles have in the African continent?" He said, "Every single issue—all of our tribal divisions; it is multiculturalism just at a different level. Every single issue you talk about is an issue we are battling with for the survival of our own continent in Africa." People in Asia have told me the same thing. The battle today is between two great world views, and we are right up on the front lines, which is why it is so important that we understand the nature of that battle.

I used the term *secular naturalism*. Let me explain. The dominant mind set in America today is secular in the sense that it is of "this age" as opposed to being eternal, which is the Christian perspective. It is naturalistic, meaning that it claims that there is a naturalistic explanation for everything. I can explain how this came to be. I can explain how we were formed. I can explain how the universe was formed. But I explain everything by natural causes; I have no need to resort to the supernatural. That world view is well formed, well established in the academy, well established in American life. It stands in complete antithesis to the biblical world view, which is biblical theism, that is, God is; He is not silent; He has spoken; He is Sovereign, the Author of all.

The alignments are Christianity versus secular naturalism; supernatural versus natural; truth versus moral relativism (what is true for you is true for you); and idealism versus pragmatism.

The biblical theistic world view says there are certain standards that ought to be. The "ought" word is so crucial. Some things ought to be. All life ought to be protected. This is antithetical to the secular world view, which is pragmatic. For example, Peter Singer, who teaches ethics at Princeton, believes in infanticide, advocates it; he believes in the greatest good or the greatest happiness for the greatest number of people—the most workable solutions. But in reality he can't live by that, because he pays large sums of money to support his own mother who has Alzheimer's. He justifies that by saying it provides work for a lot of people, so it does some good. He cannot live with his own world view.

I am going to show you that this is one of the problems with the secularist natural world view: They simply can't live with their utopianism, which says that the problem really is not in us, but it is in the world around us. As opposed to utopianism, which can't admit and talk about sin, the biblical view of life sees sin at the root of the human condition.

We look at things from an eternal perspective; the secularist looks at things from the of-this-moment perspective.

Finally, in the biblical world view, one's identity is in Christ; in the secular world view, one's identity is in an aggrieved group (on the order of left-handed transvestites, if you go far enough). It is constantly breaking culture down to find some aggrieved group with which you can find your common identity. It fragments the idea of culture or society.

Understanding the Issues

Why is it important that we understand this? Why is it so crucial? Three reasons:

Number one, you can't order your life rationally unless you understand the world view that you live by. You can't order your life rationally if you don't understand as a Christian how the world was made. C. S. Lewis put it so wonderfully. He said, "The difference between the Christian and the materialist is we hold different beliefs about the universe. They can't both be right. The one who is wrong will act in a way that simply doesn't fit the universe." This is like walking into a dark room that is full of furniture and not turning the lights on. If you don't think about the physical and moral order God has created, you are not going to live a rational life.

David Larson has told us that Christians live better, healthier, more fulfilled lives in every respect—because when you live as a Christian, you are living in accordance with the moral and physical order, the way the universe is made. You figured out the way things work, and you are living in accordance with it, which means you have discovered truth.

It is important for Christians to understand world view and cultural issues so that we can evangelize more effectively. Francis Schaeffer, to whom we owe such a debt, used to emphasize the importance of preevangelization: We must engage in cultural evangelization, because it is so hard to engage the mind of the secularist who is hardened in his views. I could walk into a room and say, "Jesus is the answer." Christians would know what I mean. But if I walk into a room of secularists and say, "Jesus is the answer," they would respond, "Well, what is the question?" Because they really don't know the question, we have got to prepare them first by explaining there is a question and then showing them what it is.

So often today as we reach across this huge divide between secular naturalism and biblical theism, we have got to prepare people by explaining that there really is a problem of the human heart that they have got to deal with. There really is a physical and moral order. There is not only a law of gravity, but there is also a moral law, and if you transgress either the physical or the moral law, you are going to be in equal trouble. We sometimes have got to explain to them the background of their own belief system.

In the book *How Now Shall We Live?* I tell the story of my meeting with the Bulgarian justice minister. To slowly bring him around so he could see the fallacy of his own world view, I explained to him what he believed and why he as a Marxist believed it. Then I could share the gospel and see a total transformation in that man's face. This illustrates that we must be prepared to engage the world in discussion—understand and articulate their world view and our own—to prepare the ground for evangelism. This is exactly what Paul did on Mars Hill.

IT IS IMPORTANT FOR CHRISTIANS TO UNDERSTAND WORLD VIEW AND CULTURAL ISSUES SO THAT WE CAN EVANGELIZE MORE EFFECTIVELY.

Third, it is absolutely essential that we understand the struggle of world views and why the biblical world view is the only answer—so that we can go into the world and contend for the truth. Is that our obligation? Of course, it is! God tells us in the creation covenant that we are to take dominion, that we are to cultivate and till, that we are to engage in the intellectual tasks of naming the animals. We are to be concerned that the glory of God be reflected in all areas of life. This involves contending for truth so that this culture, to the maximum extent possible (not that we are trying to take over), reflects the Creator because doing so pleases Him. That means we must be able to contend for truth and live out our world view. We are to go by the road map that works, that gets us to the destination we want to get to, and live accordingly, so that we impact the world around us.

I also told this story in the book—about Robby George, who teaches at Princeton University. It illustrates so well how Christians can do what they ought to do in the marketplace. Robby George teaches political science, always a packed crowd of students, a very popular course. He is a wonderful teacher. His classes cover the founding documents—the basic documents of the country—including the Declaration of Independence. In one of the classes, the first of the season, before hundreds of Princeton students, he started out by saying, "Since we are going to be speaking about the founding documents of our republic, I think we should give a moment of thanks to the Creator who made it possible for us to have these things. We do say in the Declaration of Independence, 'We hold these truths to be self-evident, that all men are created equal, that they are endowed by their Creator with certain unalienable rights, that among these are Life, Liberty, and the pursuit of Happiness.' So we will give thanks to that Creator that this is so. You can all bow your heads and pray in accordance with your own beliefs, whatever they are—your own traditions. If you don't have any belief system, that is fine, just bow your head and be glad somebody next to you does!" Everybody prayed. Heads bowed. Of course, the teaching faculty working for Robby turned around, their eyes wide open and their hair standing on end! But a professor can do this, and do so appropriately because he is talking about something that he is teaching. Many people have had similar experiences. Phillip Johnson has gone all over the United States debating Darwinists and beating them at every turn. We can do this! We can make a difference in the culture we live in if we understand what we're talking about.

Let's very briefly turn to the three philosophical questions previously mentioned and a fourth that is a consequence of the first three.

Where Do We Come From?

Where do we come from? Again, in *How Now Shall We Live?* I tell the story of Dave and Katy going to Epcot Center, to that great icon of American culture, the number-one tourist attraction in our country. The story, actually, is the experience Patty and I had, taking our then-eight-year-old grandson to Epcot Center and going to the *Living Seas* exhibit. You wait forty-five minutes in line. Nobody is having a good time; everybody is just standing in line in the sweltering heat. People with spun candy brush by you and stick their hands all over you and push and shove. Well. . .you finally get inside. There you sit in a room where you are surrounded by a screen and by sound. It is a dazzling display. All of a sudden you see stars, galaxies all around you, popping in all different directions. Then a voice comes over the PA system, which says that one small sphere happened to be just the right distance from its mother star. The scene focuses in on planet Earth. And then you hear these incredible special effects and the voice says that the molten volcanoes are exploding on planet Earth. You hear the crashing behind you and then drenching rains—caused by the volcanic heat. Then it finally shows this explosion arising up out of the sea, and the voice says that from this—the rains, the water that formed—a tiny single-cell plant captured the energy of the sun. Life began. A cosmic accident!

Eighty million people a year sit there in this dazzling display being bathed in secular naturalism! I happened to support the boycott of Disney, not so much because of their support of gay rights or their dreadful movies, but because they are soaking people in secular naturalism.

After our visit, I called the Disney representatives to complain because I watched my grandson's face through the show. His eyes were wide. I thought, *What am I doing?* I stood in this line and in the sweltering heat to get my grandson indoctrinated in secular naturalism! But that is exactly the prevailing view. Disney said, "We don't take any stands on controversial issues like God." What? They had just drummed Him out of existence at Epcot Center.

Carl Sagan popularized the *Cosmos* series on public television and in schools. He said, "The cosmos is all there is and ever will be," which, of course, doesn't answer the question, because it simply denies any question of the first cause, saying that the universe is eternal.

Then came the evidence of the big bang. Sagan promoted the eternal cosmos philosophy even after the scientists came along proclaiming that the evidence proves there really was a big bang. The scientific conclusion today is that it all began simply with a big bang. But this, of course, also misses the point completely, because how did the big bang start? Who created it? Five or six years ago there was a discovery that energy waves went out from the big bang at different intensities so that matter could form. An M.I.T. scientist appeared on TV explaining that the universe all began with a superdense ball about the size of a basketball. He said it must have been an incredible source of energy that would explode and create what is there today. Of course there was! It was God. The problem with the secular view is that it simply doesn't stand up to the evidence.

And the evidence continues to mount that there is design in the universe. Even Einstein understood this. He simply was hung up on the second major philosophic question: How could a good God be all-powerful and allow the kind of suffering that exists in the world? That, not his scientific views, kept him from belief in a personal Creator God. But he could clearly see that there was a rational mind behind this universe, that the universe and life couldn't have come about simply by accident. Famously he said, "God does not play dice with the cosmos."

In the schools, teaching of Darwinism perpetuates secular naturalism. That is what they were arguing about in Kansas. Darwinism, however, is filled with holes. There has been no case of one species becoming another—no fossil records that support this. There are all kinds of evidences of adaptation, but no evidence of one species becoming another. As a matter of fact, the more we learn, the more the evidence against Darwinism mounts. Michael Behe of Lehigh

University wrote a little book, *Darwin's Black Box,* in which he said that the basic cell structure is what he called "irreducibly complex." It is like a mousetrap. You couldn't have evolved into a mousetrap by having first a platform and then a spring and then a snap. All had to be there at once to work, and the cell is exactly like that.

The evidence is mounting that the account we find in Scripture is true, that God spoke us into being. But as you see these two arguments played out, we Christians have to be equipped to say which one is true. Lovingly, and on scientific grounds—with the best evidence available—we need to be able to persuade school boards, friends, and those who think we are simply "backwoods, Bible-pounding bigots" that secular naturalism simply isn't a rational way to order our lives. It is unlivable. It doesn't meet that first test of a world view, that is, whether it is true and conforms to the way things are.

> THE EVIDENCE IS MOUNTING THAT THE ACCOUNT WE FIND IN SCRIPTURE IS TRUE, THAT GOD SPOKE US INTO BEING.

Ask the question: Can you live with it? The answer is no. Probably the best evidence of that was Carl Sagan. All of his life he believed what he taught in his film, that we are simply products of nature. And as products of nature, we would be all the same. All products of nature are morally equivalent. We are exactly the same as animals. (In fact, we may have an obligation to care for them because we are superior to them.) So Carl Sagan always strongly believed in animal rights and all of the animal rights' causes. Sagan believed in this until he was diagnosed with a potentially fatal disease of the blood. He was told there was no cure for it, except one possible bone marrow transplant. But the doctor warned him ahead of time, "Dr. Sagan, we know exactly what you have believed all your life about medical research on animals, and we want you to know that this treatment has been developed by research on animals." Tough problem, huh? How long do you suppose it took to make his decision? Twenty seconds. You simply cannot live with that world view; it simply is not rational.

What's more, naturalism is inherently self-refuting. A naturalist believes that we arose from a cosmic accident of a chance collision of atoms that came down when light rays were refracted in a certain way and amino acid molecules spun off. They all happened to be left handed and so bonded together forming one protein cell. And here we are eight billion years later! After all these chance mutations—all breaking just right—nothing but grown-up germs! A naturalist has to arrive at the conclusion naturally in his mind. The problem is that his mind is the result of chance mutations over eight billion years of those inanimate objects that spun into life suddenly from those few initial molecules.

So how can you know that your mind—with which you are asserting this as truth—is capable of producing truth? How do you know that that chance collision could produce an intelligence that would enable you to say this with any degree of certainty? You can't. It is simply self-refuting. Naturalism fails on its own weight when you challenge it.

Why Are We in the Mess We Are In?

The second big question, *Why is there sin and suffering?* is one of the most difficult. The two world views clash fundamentally on this question of why we are in the mess we are in. How do we deal with the existence of evil?

Let me simply give the Christian view. We read from the account in Genesis that God made humans good. But He made us in His image, which means He gave us a free will. Adam and Eve disobeyed. God did not create evil, but evil arose, sin arose, from the action of Adam and Eve disobeying God. Saint Augustine made a great argument about this. There is no bad, there is simply the absence of the good that God created for us. When there is sin and suffering, it is because of the disobedience to the good that God has created. God did not create evil or cause sin. We did. And from that original sin, human nature was thereafter bent toward evil and away from the good.

If I had one Scripture passage to give to those in the culture today, it would be this: "Jesus called the crowd to him and said, 'Listen to me, everyone, and understand this. Nothing outside a man can make him 'unclean' by going into him. Rather, it is what comes out of a man that makes him 'unclean' " (Mark 7:14–16 NIV). The human condition is that there is sin within. We sin because we are sinners; we aren't sinners because we sin. Crucial distinction!

The secular view as we know it today can trace its roots to a colorful Swiss-born philosopher named Jean Jacques Rousseau who said that man is born good. And Romanticism developed from that. "Man is born free, and everywhere is in chains," Rousseau famously said. Out of that grew a utopian belief that if we could restore humans to their pristine state of goodness, freed from the corruption of society, we could create a perfect culture, and government, of course, would be the instrument to do it.

The most pernicious influence in this century, in my opinion, was Rousseau's view about the goodness of man. This, the greatest myth of the twentieth century, has led to the idea that through government we could create utopian structures. What did that mean in much of the world? It ended up in the gulag and in the "killing fields." Pol Pot was known to be reading Rousseau while he was sending Cambodians off to be slaughtered. It led to the great tyrannies of the twentieth century. In the West it led to the idea that a benevolent government could create a perfect utopian society. This in turn took away the individual's sense of self-responsibility and human dignity. I see it in the criminal justice field. From prison to prison, we see people who were told, "You are not a criminal; you are a victim of circumstances, and we are going to put you in this prison and reform you." This eroded people's understanding of their own responsibility for their own behavior.

The answer to that second question—dealing with the problem of evil—is crucial. The answer is not that we were born good; it is that we were born bent and distorted by original sin. The biblical account is correct, and Jesus' words are absolutely correct. If you get that wrong, you get everything else about your world view wrong. As a matter of fact, one great theologian said that wrong anthropology will always lead to wrong theology. It is one of the causes of liberalism within the church; it has gravely undermined culture.

Can anyone look at Littleton, Colorado, and say that evil is not real? Can anyone look at Littleton and not see the two world views in conflict? We saw kids profoundly influenced by the writings of Nietzsche (who influenced Hitler), celebrating their swastikas and their Gothic dress, killing for the joy of killing, versus a world view that celebrated life even in death, a world view that celebrated overcoming evil with good. Littleton, I believe, was the Pearl Harbor of the culture war, because it was a turning point when people could see the two world views on display. You couldn't deny the reality of evil. You couldn't deny the reality of human sin. And when you do deny it, you only compound it.

Is There a Way Out?

The third question: *Is there a way out of the human dilemma?* For me, working on this part of *How Now Shall We Live?* was probably the most enriching experience of the project. When you look at all other religions and all other world views, you see that none of them can answer this question. They all try to and fail.

Every liberation movement failed, whether it was liberation from sexual repression or liberation from all your neuroses (such as Freud trying to liberate you from all the things you had done as a child—for example, sucking your thumb too long) or Marxism liberating you from economic oppression. None of those liberation movements has succeeded.

No other religion can answer the question. I love to preach in Buddhist or Hindu countries. I talk about Jesus Christ who died on the Cross to forgive our sins and who enables us to have a new life in Him, and I watch those people's eyes come wide open. They have never heard that message before, because in the Hindu culture what you have done in this world will be done to you in the next world. It is a despairing belief system. All Eastern religions are. The Muslim hasn't any hope either. He has to walk over a perilous sword of judgment after he dies. The Jew is still waiting for the Messiah. Only the Christian knows that there is an answer to "Why do I know what is right and do what is wrong?" and knows that there is a way that guilt and sin can be removed; there is a way I can be cleansed. It's the redemptive message of Christ!

I think of Martha Williamson. She is doing exactly what C. S. Lewis said: "We don't need Christian writers; we need writers who are Christians, who get that redemptive message into people's minds and imaginations." They begin to see the value to us of the great redemptive hope in films and literature, which is what Martha does so well, being such a brilliant writer. We have got to be able to get to the world that message of redemption in words that they can understand. The central truth of the Christian life is that there is an answer to that question for all human dilemmas.

How Do We Live?

What, then, do we do when we have found that answer? Too many of us sing our hymns, our happy-clappys. We are now Christians; we have been saved, and now it is all over. No! We are saved from sin. We know the affirmative answer to the third question, "Is there a way out?" But there's more. We are saved that we may be instruments of God in restoring the world in which we live, a world that is broken and fallen and under the curse just as we are under the curse because of the Fall. Our job is to go back to the creation covenant and live in such a way that we bring restoration to the culture.

As we outline in the book, it is possible to bring Christian truth to bear on every single area of life. The workplace makes no sense if work is not invested with dignity, because it is a reflection of the Creator's gifts and is done to the glory of God. That is what gave birth to the work ethic.

Politics degenerates into shouting matches if there is no transcendent standard of good, which is the case today because of terrible decisions of the Supreme Court. In the *Casey v. Planned Parenthood* decision (being the worst), Justice Kennedy defined liberty as the right to define one's own concept of existence or meaning. So the law loses its transcendent base of authority, and it thus becomes only an instrument of coercion.

Music, art, culture—they no longer have meaning if there are not absolutes of beauty and truth to which they can aspire and lift people. Art becomes whatever someone says it is. The virgin Mary, with dung hung on the picture. Is that art? Of course not. Maybe free speech, but it is not art.

In every area of life you see that Christian truth provides a better road map for the way to live. We can't sit back and enjoy our faith when there is a great struggle going on. It isn't just a culture war. It isn't just over the issues that are so common to us. It is a struggle for the hearts and minds of six billion people on planet Earth. We can't sit back when we understand the framework of a biblical world view and see how it plays out in all of life. We can't just sit back and enjoy what we have.

OUR JOB IS TO GO BACK TO THE CREATION COVENANT AND LIVE IN SUCH A WAY THAT WE BRING RESTORATION TO THE CULTURE.

We have to live it out and persuade our neighbors that the truth of the biblical world view provides a more rational way for them to order their lives. It provides the only way in which a society can truly live together, in which good can overcome evil, as we saw in Littleton. It provides the only hope that there is an answer to the human dilemma that is within us. It is the only world view that makes sense of the way things are—as they really are. That is the test of truth. Is something true? Does it conform to reality? Does it record the way things are? Yes. Once you understand that and see Christianity this way, you can then live your life differently in a way that will make an impact on the culture around you. You can then persuade the people with whom God puts you in contact that there is truth and that you can pursue it.

What a glorious opportunity as the millennium dawns! What a time for us to live this world view! What a time to take the kind of stand taken by William Wilberforce in his day, taken by the saints down through the ages, as "all truth is God's truth" is proclaimed broadly and widely throughout the world by God's people who know it and defend it and live it out!

God bless you!

C. S. Lewis: The Prophet
of the Twentieth Century

Cambridge, England
August, 1998

My task today is to talk about C. S. Lewis as the great prophet of this century that I believe he, along with Francis Schaeffer, indeed was. But before I do, I hope you will indulge me a bit of personal reflection.

Lewis's personal influence is something of a convergence of history this particular week, because twenty-five years ago this very day—in a flood of tears, in a friend's driveway, in the toughest days of my life, in the midst of the darkest days of Watergate—I surrendered my life to Christ. It is no accident that I am here today on the one hundredth anniversary of the birth of C. S. Lewis, for it was his writing that convicted me. Would I have been converted without Lewis? Yes. I am enough of a five-point Calvinist of reformed theology to believe that God had His hooks in me and would have gotten me. The Hound of Heaven would have pursued me, as Lewis wrote, but it was Lewis whom God used to convict me. I had succeeded in everything that I had done in my life. I was the youngest company commander in the U.S. Marine Corps, the youngest administrative assistant in the U.S. Senate, the youngest this and that, and I had started a big, successful law firm. I was the youngest senior aide to the president of the United States. I thought I was so good. I never thought about being a sinner. I always thought I wasn't any worse than anyone else; I hadn't done anything the Democrats hadn't done before me; and God, like any good college professor, would grade on a curve, and I would be fine. Lewis convicted me so deeply with words that I am sure you are so familiar with—words from *Mere Christianity:* "There is no fault which makes a man more unpopular, and no fault which we are more unconscious of in ourselves. And the more we have it ourselves, the more we dislike it in others. The vice I am talking of is Pride. . . ."

Lewis also wrote that when you walk through life looking up toward God, you come up against something immeasurably greater than yourself. But a proud man who is always walking through life looking down on other people cannot see something, something immeasurably superior, above himself. Lewis, I am sure, did not realize that he was writing for Chuck Colson in the darkest days of Watergate. His words were like a torpedo that hit a ship. Confronted with his words, I could not even get the keys into the ignition of the automobile—I was crying too hard. There I was, a proud, ex-marine captain, White House hatchet man, calling out to God! I wanted to know Him. I didn't know the words. I had never known anything about evangelicalism. All I knew was that that night I desperately wanted to know the living God. I desperately wanted my sins lifted from me. I desperately wanted to know what this man was writing about.

That next week I went to the coast of Maine on a holiday with my wife, Patty, to get away from all the agonies of Watergate. I took *Mere Christianity* with me and read it cover to cover. I took a yellow pad, which I am want to do as a lawyer, and I made my columns: There is a God/There isn't a God; Jesus Christ is God/He isn't God. I went through the book and came against an intellect as formidable as any I had faced in my life of politics or law—the mind of C. S. Lewis. I became convinced of the truth that Jesus Christ is God.

As I said, I'm sure the Hound of Heaven would have gotten hold of me anyway, but C. S. Lewis did two things for me. First, he convicted me of my sin. He made me understand that I had to repent, and that I could be forgiven. And he gave me an intellectual framework to understand what had happened to me in that emotional experience of surrender. I was somebody who distrusted emotion. I relied on reason. I was trained as a lawyer to think analytically. And yet I was able to understand what God had done that evening, because in *Mere Christianity*, Lewis laid it out in an intellectually understandable way.

> "THE MORE WE HAVE
> IT OURSELVES,
> THE MORE WE DISLIKE IT IN OTHERS.
> THE VICE I AM TALKING
> OF IS PRIDE. . . ."
> C. S. LEWIS

This taught me a lesson that I have used in my ministry ever since. Although apologetics and reason will not lead someone to God, they will at least set the stage whereby that person can understand what is happening in his or her heart when God is moving in that life. Apologetics is necessary to set the framework for us to understand the reality of the Christian experience. This is particularly so in this age when all truths are considered equal, when there is no truth, when there is nothing to base it upon, when the Christian memory is being erased from our culture.

It is particularly vital that we be able to defend the faith and give rational and reasonable explanations for it. Because, although reason will never bring you to Christianity, Christ and the Christian faith are not unreasonable. They can be understood in an intellectual context.

Not a day goes by without my giving thanks to God for my salvation. I don't believe I have gotten up in the morning in the last twenty-five years without thanking Him for what He did in that driveway. And I can hardly think of that moment without feeling gratitude for C. S. Lewis at the same time.

Over those twenty-five years, a treasured possession has consistently reminded me of C. S. Lewis. When I came to Oxford in 1977, and spent a wonderful day speaking at the Oxford Debating Society, Walter Hooper met me. At the end of the day, he gave me a box. In that box was something wrapped up in paper. He handed it to me as I was leaving, and he said, "I want you to take this back with you and not open it until you get to London." Well, I couldn't resist! I opened it on the way back in the car, and in it was a pipe with tobacco in it—and not just any pipe. As Hooper wrote in his letter to me, "I hope you will accept this gift, one of C. S. Lewis's pipes that is now yours to do with as you like. It will interest you to know that C. S. L. left us before he had a chance to knock it out." I have it encased in glass, across from my desk. I realized that this was a pipe apparently on Lewis's desk the day he died. I was so proud of that. Every time I had a friend come to my house, I would say, "Let me show you C. S. Lewis's pipe." Mark Hatfield, the former senator, was over at my house one night, and I showed it to him. He looked at it with a sort of scorn, and said, "It may have been the one that killed him!"

There are some great ironies in the way Lewis has impacted this century—great ironies in terms of my own life. Isn't it amazing that it would be someone from outside of the Evangelical subculture who would reach the White House hatchet man? I had been at every Evangelical gathering that Richard Nixon had hosted (and Evangelicals were flowing in and out of the Nixon White House all the time), yet even though I had listened to all of those messages, nothing ever got to me. Isn't it ironic?

Isn't it ironic that Lewis would affect me as he did, and then my book would come out in 1976, the "Year of the Evangelical," as *Newsweek* labeled it in its headline? There was Jimmy Carter, a born again Christian, and that year, *Mere Christianity* enjoyed a resurgence of sales in America. Could Lewis have ever imagined that through his writings and his life of reflection he would create one of the Evangelical resurgences in our country in the later part of the twentieth century? Could he, this humble professor at Oxford and Cambridge, have imagined the supreme irony that his writings might be used to convert someone who would go on to start a ministry that is in eighty-three countries around the world reaching out to hundreds and thousands of the lost and suffering—the least of these, the people who are marginalized, off in the prisons? The lesson in that, of course, is a profound one for all of us: Whatever God has called you to do, do it with excellence. Don't jump ahead and try to imagine how you can change the world, because you can't possibly outguess God, because He has a better sense of humor than you or I do! Look what He did with C. S. Lewis's life.

Lewis and Justice

Indeed, my ministry has been profoundly shaped by Lewis's essay, "The Humanitarian Theory of Punishment."

When I got out of prison, I was aware of two things. First of all (and I had to repent for it), I realized that all of those speeches I helped Nixon write on law and order saying "lock them up and throw away the key" were wrong. (I did help him write them, at least the more eloquent ones.) I knew they were wrong, because I met people who had been in prison seven, eight times, and prison didn't deter them. I saw people who had been brought into prison on the humanitarian, utopian myth of the twentieth century that we can put people in institutions, and we can somehow rehabilitate them. I saw how false that was.

I couldn't put it together until I read "The Humanitarian Theory of Punishment." In 1954, Lewis argued so brilliantly that punishment should be based on just deserts, an understanding of what justice is—not on some therapeutic notion, not the triumph of psychology and therapy over law and reality. No, a person is punished because he has done something wrong. And only this view of punishment respects that person's humanity and dignity, because he is given "just deserts" instead of having some Viennese scientists in white coats, as he put it, in a laboratory deciding how we can either cure or deter that person's behavior.

Lewis profoundly affected my own views of capital punishment. I was opposed to capital punishment most of my life until I really understood the just deserts theory and realized that there are some cases that warrant capital punishment. This realization came when I was visiting John Wayne Gacy on death row in Menard, Illinois. He was so totally unrepentant, I realized that there was nothing else that would respect his humanity other than the just deserts of punishment.

Lewis saw where the "humanitarian theory" would lead us to, and that brings me to our topic. Lewis saw this at a time when Eisenhower was in the White House talking about peace, progress, and prosperity; when Ozzie and Harriet had moved into Levittown; when Britain was rebuilding after the war; when everybody was at peace; when everybody was comfortable because life was back to normal. Lewis saw that it wasn't anywhere near normal. The prophet, the visionary, sees that which others can't see. What he saw was more than just the flaws in the justice system. He saw the triumph of therapy over responsibility. He saw the utopian's conquest, the victory of psychology and biology and science over law and reality. He saw how our traditional social consensus was coming unraveled.

> "A TYRANNY
> SINCERELY EXERCISED FOR
> THE GOOD OF ITS VICTIMS
> MAY BE THE MOST
> OPPRESSIVE OF ALL."
> C. S. LEWIS

When we drop the concept of just deserts, the only two questions we can ask about punishment are whether it deters crime or whether it cures. But these aren't questions on which any ordinary man has judgment, as Lewis argued; what is likely to deter crime is a question that only an expert penologist can answer; what is likely to cure is a question only the psychotherapists can answer. So take away the notion of the just dessert, and the whole morality of punishment disappears. "Why, in heaven's name," he asked, "am I [someone charged with a crime] to be sacrificed to the good of society in this way, unless, of course, I deserve it?" Here's what Lewis said—this is when he was beginning to speak so powerfully about what was happening to our culture: "My contention is that good men, not bad men, consistently acting upon the humanitarian theory of punishment would act as cruelly and unjustly as the greatest tyrants of all tyranny. A tyranny sincerely exercised for the good of its victims may be the most oppressive of all."

He then goes on to suggest that religion could be considered a neurosis—and just think how people could treat Christians if religion were considered a neurosis. This is precisely, of course, what happened in the Soviet Union. And this is precisely what is happening in totalitarian countries all around the world today—and precisely what could very easily happen if we don't have the courage in Western society to defend a traditional, morally rooted world view. Today it is merely impolite to talk about Christian truth, but in the not-too-distant future it may be considered a sign of mental unbalance.

Why Did Lewis "See"?

Lewis turns out to be the keenest prophet of the twentieth century. But why do you suppose he saw these things? How odd that it would be a professor of medieval literature! One can only speculate why it is so. I have one theory: He saw the signs of the changing times—the vacant stare of the coming postmodernism—written on the faces of young students in the classrooms before him. He heard in his students' questions the beginnings of deconstructionism, depriving words of their meaning. What counted was not that Coleridge's waterfall was really sublime, but whether that tourist thought it was sublime. I think Lewis saw the mood on the faces of students, when politicians and other cultural elites could not see it in the generation of leaders.

Maybe it was because Lewis understood the power of the imagination and how our aesthetic senses affect the way we ultimately think. This is why I am so appreciative of all of the artists and poets and authors who have been here this week to remind us of the need to reach out with the truth, not only propositionally to the mind, but to all of the senses as well. I know Lewis understood.

Or maybe it was because, as a scholar, Lewis had a well-formed

and referred to some of these concepts, I was chided by students who said I was using terms like *naturalism* and *positivism* and *materialism* and *relativism* without putting them in context. So let me give a very simplistic snapshot of the course of Western thought against which we have to understand what Lewis saw and predicted. This will be terribly beneath most of you in this crowd. I guess this is a sign of the times. We take philosophy today and reduce it to a bumper sticker, don't we? So I give you a story of Western culture on a bumper sticker.

From the Greeks onward, Western culture generally embraced the idea of a transcendent, absolute moral order. The Greeks believed in the absolutes of truth, beauty, and justice. They believed that a well-ordered life was a life lived in accord with these things. Then came the rise of Christianity and the belief in Judeo-Christian truth rooted in revelation. The "God who has spoken, who is" spoke to us, and those words shaped our belief system. Science became possible only because of that belief formed by the Judeo-Christian tradition; science is only measuring what is, what is real. If there is no order, no absolute order, what is there to measure? You can't measure chaos. So science and the whole pursuit of knowledge rested upon these foundations.

Dramatic change in Western thought came about in the seventeenth century. I'll use as my dividing point when René Descartes retreated to the isolation of what might be called his "Dutch oven"—that famous moment—because he couldn't decide what was real in the world. So he sat in his Dutch oven until he decided what was real. And when he came out, he decided *cogito ergo sum,* "I think, therefore I am." The only thing he was sure was real was the fact that he could think. Although he was a strong believer himself, that phrase had profound and dangerous implications for the West, because it got people thinking of reality not in terms of what is external to us and objective and transcendent, but rather in terms of how we perceive it. Truth became a subjective matter. Not coincidentally, the introduction of subjectivity into knowing reality came the Enlightenment passion for the rights of man. The idea took hold that God was no longer needed to explain the cosmos, and therefore God was no longer needed for moral formulation. Along came Kant, who said that if we can't perfectly empirically validate something, we can't really know that it is. And finally we arrived at Nietzsche, who went beyond Kant and said that if you can't validate something, it isn't. So, "God is dead."

Naturalism, the idea that there is a naturalistic explanation for everything, became a predominant theme of the Enlightenment. But it didn't become part of popular Western consciousness until the twentieth century. John Dewey took naturalistic principles and transformed education from the pursuit of knowledge of an absolute truth and moral truth into a process. Justice Oliver Wendell Holmes took these concepts and said that the law is no longer a binding set of transcendent truths—it is merely what sociologists think will work best for the people. Then there was Freud, in the 1920s, with his preoccupation with the therapeutic approach to life. And of course there was Darwin, whose naturalistic theory that we have evolved and are merely the highest form of primates has become so popularized.

Paul Johnson, the great British popular historian, marks the dividing era of modern times with Einstein's discovery of relativity in 1919. People latched onto the word *relativity*, confusing relativism in the realm of ideas with relativity in the physical sciences.

Relativism, the idea that all propositions are morally equal and that there is no binding objective transcendent truth, and naturalism (or materialism), the idea that there is a naturalistic explanation for everything, have become dominant in today's culture.

Traditional Western thought fought a valiant fight for a long time—even into the middle of the twentieth century. When I studied at Brown University in the early fifties, I took a course in sociology.

Just to show you how quickly things have changed in the academy, that semester course in sociology was all about the traditional father and mother—the heterosexual family—and how that family worked. Today at Brown you can get your major in gay and lesbian studies. That is all in less than half a century.

An Unfolding Prophetic Vision

But Lewis saw where naturalism and relativism would lead. In his first book, *Pilgrim's Regress,* published in 1933, he saw the utter sterility of materialism or naturalism as an idea. His allegorical everyman, John, had to pass on his journey through the deception of materialism. And he mocked it! I love the way Lewis did this! He mocked it, dismissing it as "a philosophy for boys." Wonderful! For Lewis, Christianity and Hinduism are the only two serious options for the adult mind.

Three works, to which I would like to refer briefly, capture his prophetic vision for what was happening to the latter half of the twentieth century: *The Abolition of Man,* in 1943, (which includes my favorite essay of all time, "Men Without Chests"); "The Poison of Subjectivism," also written in 1943; and "Miracles," an article that first appeared in 1942, and again later in book form in 1947. In these three writings we see his prophetic vision unfold.

First, he exposed the inherent irrationality of materialism. The job of the good apologist is always to start with our presupposition, God is: He has spoken; He has created the universe; He has spoken it into existence. And a good apologist demonstrates that any other proposition is irrational. This is precisely what Lewis did. Materialism gives us a theory which explains everything else in the whole universe, but which makes it impossible to believe that our thinking is valid. That's because an accident cannot think of itself in any objective sense. Consider Lewis's words: "In order to think, we must claim for our reasoning a validity which is not credible if our own thought is merely a function of our brain, and our brains are a by-product of irrational, physical processes." Precisely! Every one of you can handle an argument with materialist, naturalist friends, who say there is a naturalistic explanation for everything. How can they know what they are saying is true? They are making their claim with a brain that supposedly results from a chance collision of atoms that came out of the primordial soup eight billion years ago.

Then Lewis showed how this irrational materialism would lead to the death of morality. "This thing which I have called for the sake of convenience Tao, and which others may call Natural Law, or Traditional Morality, or the First Principles of Practical Reason, or the First Platitudes, is not one of a series of possible systems of value. It is the sole source of all value judgments. If it is rejected, all value is rejected." He went on to say, as an illustration of this, "Therefore if I say, 'I ought,' that has no greater moral weight than if I were to say, 'I itch.'" Exactly! He saw that relativism was taking the law apart. The whole attempt to jettison traditional values as something subjective and substitute a new scheme of values for them is wrong. It is like trying to lift yourself by your own coat collar. I love that illustration, because if you try to lift yourself by your own coat collar, you will not only fail to lift yourself, you will only succeed at choking and strangling yourself in the process. This is precisely what modern man is doing. Francis Schaeffer said it well: "The modern man has both feet planted firmly in midair."

Lewis saw that a world view founded on materialistic principles could allow no room for ethics. I have lectured on ethics (or the lack of them) at several great universities in America, and I never can get any kind of debate going with the students. They have lost the language with which they can even engage in moral discourse, because they have been so enmeshed in this idea that there can be no absolute truth.

We can't even communicate today, because we have deconstructed, or taken apart, the meaning of language. Lewis saw this coming in "Men Without Chests" published in 1943, in which he described the reaction to Coleridge's example of the waterfall; those who said it was sublime were not saying that it was sublime in reality, but rather that they saw it as sublime. Lewis called this, in another essay, "verbicide," the killing of words by stripping away and perverting meaning. If there is no objective meaning, I might say, "This is so" (because of x, y, z), and you would be perfectly at liberty to respond, "That is all right, you can believe that," because that is only the way you see it. Nothing we say conveys the truth about anything other than the way we feel.

WE CAN'T EVEN COMMUNICATE TODAY, BECAUSE WE HAVE DECONSTRUCTED. . . THE MEANING OF LANGUAGE.

I have often lectured on the death of the rule of law. When I told the students at Yale Law School that their school was responsible for law's demise because the "school of critical legal studies" (deconstructionism) was born there, I thought I might start a riot. But they didn't argue with me, because they have rejected the law of noncontradiction. I can believe one thing, and they can believe something absolutely antithetical, and we can both be right! Utterly preposterous! But that is what deconstruction does. And it has affected literature, it has affected education, the law, and every area of life.

But Lewis saw where all of this would lead us. In "The Humanitarian Theory of Punishment," he said it would give rise to the great utopian pretensions. Deconstructionism opens the door to the great myth of the twentieth century: The goodness of man—that good people, freed of prudish Victorian restraints, can live in perfect bliss. But since it is the "controllers" who deliver us from such restraints, it in fact leads to the smoldering ashes of Auschwitz and the flowing rivers of blood in the Cambodian killing fields. The disaster of the twentieth century was the belief that man is good and can create his own utopia. Lewis saw this ever so clearly, as he wrote in *The Abolition of Man:* "Let us decide for ourselves what man is to be and make him into that, not from any ground of imagined value, but because we want him to be such; having mastered our environment, let us now master ourselves and choose our own destiny. Man's final conquest has proved to be the abolition of man."

Subjectivism leads to tyranny. "The very idea of freedom," Lewis wrote in "The Poison of Subjectivism," "presupposes some objective moral order which overarches both ruler and ruled alike. Subjectivism about values is eternally incompatible with democracy. We and our rulers are of one kind only so long as we are subject to one law, but if there is no law of nature, the ethos of any society is the creation of its rulers, educators, and conditioners, and every creator stands outside his own creation."

That expresses precisely the dilemma of the postmodern age. And remember who the barbarians are. The barbarians come, Lewis told us, not over the parapet, not carrying their clubs and wielding their weapons, but they come with polished fingernails and blue pinstripe suits, gathering in well-lighted conference rooms. They are the good people who say that they know how to make life better for all of us.

Before I tell you what I think we should do with all of this, I must point out one other irony. It's rather overwhelming, as a matter of fact. During World War II, when the entire world was mobilized in the great confrontation between the Allies and the Axis;

when Roosevelt and Churchill lifted the world to heroic exertions in protection and defense of liberty and freedom; when the world was seen as polar (good versus evil); when that war was seen as the war to end all wars and the war to make the world safe for democracy; when blood was being shed horrifically; when the whole world believed it was confronting the greatest evil; it wasn't confronting the greatest evil. All the while, a quiet professor, sipping a pint, reading his beloved books, saw the true struggle differently. He saw the titanic struggle of good and evil not so much between the armies of the Axis and the Allies; he saw it in the workings of the human heart and the mind.

In prison, Solzhenitsyn put it so wonderfully: "The line between good and evil passes not between principalities and powers, but through every human heart, and it oscillates back and forth." Lewis understood that. Lewis saw that the virus that gave rise to a Hitler was an alien idea, the embodiment of what Nietzsche had predicted would happen in his "will to power"—the superman. That same virus was infecting the good people here in Cambridge and Oxford and in Washington and in Boston. The battle lines were not necessarily drawn at Normandy and Omaha Beach and Dunkirk and Anzio, but in the world of ideas, in answering the question: "How now shall we live?" He understood that in the war over truth, the battle being fought was naturalism versus supernaturalism. And that is the battle we fight today. How now shall we deal with that issue? How now shall we live?

How Shall We Live?

I have four thoughts to leave with you this day as to how to answer that question.

The first is that despair is sin. There is never, never, never an excuse for a Christian to despair. We know how the final battle between good and evil has been fought and won—at Golgotha, with victory assured. We await the final culmination of history. This truth that Lewis grasped allowed him to be positively sanguine about the state of affairs. Not a pacifist—he always believed in doing one's duty—but at peace. He said, in effect, "What are we worrying about? The world's coming to an end anyway! History has been written already by our Creator. If it goes up in a puff of smoke, it goes up in a puff of smoke, or it goes up when you simply keel over and that's the end of things. What is the difference?" He would have laughed at all of the apocalyptic predictions and movies like *Armageddon*. They would amuse him if he saw them today.

THERE IS NEVER, NEVER, NEVER AN EXCUSE FOR A CHRISTIAN TO DESPAIR.

The twenty-first century can be the great Christian century, if we understand that every other single way of perceiving reality, every other single possible world view, every explanation of what is, has been proven false and fraudulent and bankrupt and lies in the rubble of the Berlin Wall, in the dustbin of history. If only Christians have the sense to grab this moment and offer hope to the world, to say, "Yes, Christianity is the only rational explanation, the only way people can live their lives." Then this can be a moment not of despair, even as postmodernity seems to swallow us up. This is not a moment of despair. It is a moment of opportunity.

Second, I will say something that is controversial. I know it is controversial, because I have said it in small groups this week and already had people taking exception to it. There is nothing more important than that we be "mere Christians"—it is the first line of defense as we enter the new millennium. What Lewis meant by this phrase is that while there are many differences among us—Catholic, Orthodox, fifty-seven varieties of Protestantism—we live in the same house. We discuss our differences, when we have them, as we emerge from our rooms. We do live in separate rooms, because we understand our faith in different ways, but basically we agree on the fundamentals of the Christian faith. But it is inside the house that we ought to have those disagreements among ourselves. The problem today is supernaturalism versus naturalism.

True Christians—those who believe in the substitutionary atonement of the Cross, who believe that Jesus Christ is, indeed, Lord, that He died for our sins, that He calls us to come before Him in repentance and to give our lives to Him and follow Him as Lord—must lock arms and stand together against the forces of naturalism. We must do this not only to defeat those forces, but also to share in the glorious witness to the risen Christ. And we do it by standing together as Christians, not by being divided among ourselves. If we remain divided, it will be a sin before our Lord who prayed for the church: "Father, may they be one with one another, as I am One with You in order that the world will know that You have sent Me" (see John 17:23). How can the world know that Jesus was sent by the Father when the world sees nothing but Christians fighting among themselves?

We will never achieve unity in my lifetime, but I intend to devote my lifetime to working toward it—not in disregard of truth but in service of truth, realizing that it is the condition that God has created while division is the condition that man has created. And no one understood this better than the one who called us to be "mere Christians."

Third, if we see one thing from the life and writings of C. S. Lewis, we see the necessity for Christians to have a well-formed world view. I think Lewis saw these things because he came from the intellectual world. He understood the intellectual history of Western civilization. He was able to put Christianity in context. Christianity is more than John 3:16. It is more than, "I have come before the Father, and I am now saved—hallelujah. Now I will go back to my church and study my Bible." Christianity is more than that; it is the truth that God created this universe, and everything is under His sovereign judgment. And Christians are to bring to bear this truth in every single area of life, from arts and science and literature and music, to politics and anthropology, right across the entire board; and that means understanding Christian truth that is lived out and made incarnate in every aspect of life. Lewis understood this. This is what enables us to be good apologists.

Why do we care about world view? We care about world view because we can't live rationally without one. It would be like somebody going into a dark room filled with furniture and not turning the lights on. My friend Cornelius Plantinga at Calvin College says sin is nothing but folly; it is stupidity. It is not looking at and ordering your lives according to the moral order the way God has created the moral order. And so you are constantly "cutting against the grain of the universe" or, as he puts it so graphically, "spitting into the wind." And that is what so many of us do. We truncate Christianity. We cut it short. We don't see it as a world-view system in conflict with other world-view systems. And we don't live it out, because we don't understand that it is more than simply "I am saved. You are saved. We are okay." It is much more; it is the way we apprehend reality.

A Christian world view gives us the ability not only to order our lives rationally; it gives us the ability to evangelize. As I said earlier, I believe I would have been converted had I not read *Mere Christianity*, but *Mere Christianity* put it all in an intellectual context.

Remember, we are to advance Christian truth in two ways: to

defend it as apologists and to be instruments of common grace. Every one of us should be an instrument of common grace. God in His saving grace reaches down, and He converts and He transforms the heart. But He also reaches down and holds back the flood of sin that would otherwise engulf us. He uses us as His instruments, and He uses nonbelievers as His instruments of common grace to sustain His creation. Remember, defend and live the truth, and save us from tyranny.

And finally, I would urge that we realize that, in the final analysis, the battle is not ours. The battle is the Lord's. I have listened to talks this week that have moved me so deeply. Every single one of us has an agenda. I do, of course. Everybody who has spoken from this pulpit has an agenda. But I think the time comes when we set aside man's agenda and man's programs, when we decrease that He might increase, when we realize that it is God, a holy God, whom we serve. We put ourselves aside. We fall prostrate before Him, and we say "You are the King of Kings. Use us where You will. Use us in any way You choose."

Because in the final analysis only one thing matters, that is, as Lewis put it so wonderfully: "When the Lord returns, it matters not whether we are in a great crusade to free the slaves or whether we are tending the pigs. The important thing," he said, "is that we would be found at our posts." What did Lewis expect of Christians when Christ returns? Simply that we be at our posts, doing our duty.

Why do we do our duty? Out of gratitude to God. G. K. Chesterton said, "The mother of all virtues is gratitude." We do it out of gratitude to God for what He has done in our lives. So putting aside our own desires, putting aside our petty and partisan differences, putting aside our prejudices, deciding that we are going to stand together, loving one another, arms locked, let us go out of here from this magnificent, marvelous, rich, fulfilling conference with our minds renewed, our hearts on fire, and with our wills determined at whatever cost, with courage, to stand at our posts and to do our duty in what may be the greatest season of Christian evangelism and the greatest harvest of all time as we approach the new millennium.

God bless you.

The Springtime of Harvest and the Evangelical Impulse

Erasmus Lecture
Institute for Religion in Public Life
New York, New York
November, 1999

The church may well be entering a great season of spiritual renewal, what Pope John Paul II calls in "Redemptoris Missio" the "Springtime of Evangelization."

The dawn of a new millennium finds us at what some have called, the "modernist impasse." During the past generation, as the writings of European existentialist philosophers swept across this country, people began to believe that the ultimate object in life was personal autonomy. The "do your own thing" mentality gripped us in the sixties, was translated into a variety of slogans in the seventies and the eighties, and has emerged in its extreme form as an individualism that's become our supreme value. This passion for autonomy is responsible for many of the social pathologies that plague our nation. It has even affected our understanding of law, and profoundly so.

We now see that the 1973 *Roe v. Wade* decision was about much more than abortion. It was about the Supreme Court of the United

States finding in the Constitution an implied right to privacy that extinguished the moral debate going on in all fifty state legislatures. That decision has led to innumerable judicial excesses ever since, in which the judiciary has taken more and more of the rights of self-government away from the people—all in the name of a right of privacy, that is, personal autonomy.

THIS OBSESSION FOR AUTONOMY HAS CREATED UTTER CHAOS.

This obsession with personal autonomy has now been enshrined in law, specifically, in the 1992 *Casey v. Planned Parenthood* decision. In words written by Justice Kennedy, but which might as well have been written by Jacques Derrida, the Court handed out the following: "Liberty is defined as the right to define one's own concept of existence, of being, of the universe and of the mystery of human life." This passion for personal autonomy has brought modern life to a depressing state, a condition that was never more eloquently described than by Richard Neuhaus, who wrote in the *Wall Street Journal* that we are like herds of independent minds marching toward moral oblivion with Frank Sinatra's witless boast on our lips, "I did it my way."

This obsession for autonomy has created utter chaos. For example, it has led us to a sexual epidemic. Three quarters of a million Americans today are infected with AIDS. It has led us to brutal violence, and the rampant fatherlessness that is at the root of so many of our social pathologies. I've been in six hundred prisons across America; I've looked in the faces of these kids, and I have watched them over twenty-five years of ministry. Those faces have changed. Twenty-five years ago, you could talk about God the Father, and at least those kids had a frame of reference for what you were talking about. Today, God the "Father" is a bad word. I've seen the anger in the eyes and the lack of any real conscience. The conscience that Scripture tells us we are born with is in these kids horribly malformed, for it has no basis on which to be properly formed. Augustine had it right: The desire for autonomy is "a deadly corrosive for the soul."

Unmitigated love of autonomy has led us to one of the most galvanizing contemporary events. It will be recorded by historians as the Columbine High School tragedy. I have called it the Pearl Harbor of the culture wars, because suddenly people have been caught up short. They thought that they had an adequate world view, a secular modern world view that gave them all the freedom and liberty they could want. But all of a sudden they discovered that the wonderful fruits of that world view have produced tragedy. They saw on display at Littleton two fundamentally opposed world views. On the one hand, they saw Eric Harris and Dylan Klebold, self-professed disciples of Hitler, himself a disciple of Nietzsche, who proclaimed the news that God is dead, denied the reality of evil, and celebrated a radical will to power. But at the same time people saw that world view on public display, they saw the world view of two girls, Rachel Scott and Cassie Bernall, who would not deny their faith and were gunned down in cold blood. And then for a week thereafter, the world saw on every news broadcast those incredible church services, both Protestant and Catholic, which exalted Jesus, featured parents forgiving the slayers of their children, and showed what was almost a celebration of the lives of those kids killed by their classmates. Columbine forced the culture to look at those two world views, displayed in vivid relief, and choose which way they will live. It was as if God were saying, as He did to His people of old, "I have set before you life and death. Choose life."

It can no longer be said that the Religious Right is attempting to cram its views down the throats of an unwilling people. Rather, people are becoming eager to listen to something more reasonable and more rational as a way of life than what led to Columbine. There is evidence that the culture is beginning to change even before our very eyes, as postmodernism sags into cultural implosion.

Just look at the indicators. Crime, for one, is today down to pre-1973 levels. Part of that can be explained by demographics, part by the huge explosion of prison construction that now accommodates 1.9 million people in America's prisons and jails, and part of it by the kind of community policing that New York City, among others, has adopted. But these alone do not fully account for the changes we are seeing.

Welfare has been cut in half, and the percentage of the population on the public dole is the lowest since 1967. The divorce rate is down 19 percent since 1980. Teenage pregnancies are down 12 percent since 1991. The number of sexually active teenagers in high schools has declined for two years in a row. Abortions are down 15 percent since 1990, despite the regime of the most pro-abortion president in our history.

The nation's moral discourse is changing as well. Just over a year and a half ago, I participated in one of those programs which gathers talking heads around a table in Washington, D.C., to dispense their wisdom to the great unwashed masses outside of the Beltway. There were six of us around the table, and when it was my turn to say something, I suggested that the inner city crisis was basically a moral problem. Suddenly, there was an awkward silence. The host looked at me as if I'd just arrived from some distant planet. After a nervous cough or two and a lengthy pause during which no one said anything, a woman two seats away from me finally piped up saying, "Yes, that's why we built a new community center here in D.C." They just didn't get it; they didn't understand what I was talking about. And yet it wasn't a year later that I was on every major talk show explaining what moral reformation is, what repentance is, and why private morality has public consequences.

The polls indicate that people want something different. Right after Columbine, a *Wall Street Journal*/NBC poll asked about the values of American life. Eighty-four percent of those who described themselves as conservative, and 33 percent of those who described themselves as liberal agreed that a priority of contemporary America was to promote respect for traditional values. What was frequently a pejorative term just months earlier has now become something both conservatives and a large minority of liberals would identify as a national priority. In the same poll, 58 percent said youth violence was the number-one social issue, and 76 percent said they favored federal funding for faith-based solutions to public policy problems. This is evidence of a profound shift taking place in our nation's values.

We're witnessing the coming of what Prof. Russell Hittinger describes as the death throes of modernity. We're seeing its dying gasps, as people are recognizing that the prevailing value system of the past forty years simply doesn't work. This is what provides those of us who believe in a Judeo-Christian world view, believing Jews and Christians of all confessions (and, I would add, moral conservatives who draw their moral views from the accumulated wisdom of Western Civilization), such an extraordinary opportunity to reshape the culture.

As we begin the new millennium, we in the Christian community can learn from our common history how best to approach this great opportunity. I'm thinking specifically of the example of Erasmus, who sought to create a network of like-minded scholars from across Europe with the hope that, together, on the foundation of truth, they would be able to restore a moral consensus and save Western culture from sectarianism, nationalism, and superstition. Erasmus crossed confessional lines and intellectual disciplines in his effort to renew moral life on the continent, publishing the works of a wide range of scholars from many nations.

Although Erasmus did not succeed in his project, still, his strategy is crucial for us today. Like Erasmus, we must, in every discipline, in many and varied contexts, and with a spirit of mutual love and encouragement, reach across confessional divides and begin together to present a rational and biblical view of life that can reach our desperate neighbors and transform our culture. This is precisely what is needed as we enter the new millennium—not just for the sake of the church, but for the greater good of mankind.

> IF WE ARE TO PERSUADE A
> HUNGERING WORLD THAT
> OUR VIEW OF REALITY IS TRUE,
> WE MUST BE PREPARED TO ADVANCE
> OUR CASE IN BOTH WORD AND DEED
> AND TO PRESENT A SOUND
> CULTURAL APOLOGETIC.

What must we do to make our case for Christian truth? What is our challenge as we approach the new millennium?

First, Christians must understand that faith in Jesus Christ is much more than a matter of personal conversion and salvation (the heart of the Evangelical faith); and it is much more than liturgy (a principal focus of the Roman Catholic faith). Christianity is a world view. It is a way of comprehending all of reality by seeing all of life through God's eyes. It affects every single aspect of life; it isn't simply a matter of, "I'm saved, you're saved, and we're okay." It is a matter of

God, Creator of all, being Sovereign over all. As Abraham Kuyper, the great Dutch theologian and political leader, put it, "There is not one square inch in the whole domain of our human existence over which Christ, who is Sovereign, does not cry out, 'Mine!' " Christians must recognize this in order to know the fullness of life in Christ, to be able to formulate a defense of Christian truth in every single area of life, and to begin taking back our culture in the name of the King of Kings.

Next, we must understand that the great battle going on in the world today is not the culture war. Rather, it is a cosmic struggle over first principles, as Kuyper also recognized. At root are competing answers to the question of how we understand reality itself. This issue turns on the question of origins. On the one hand, secular naturalism argues for a materialistic explanation for the origin of the universe, the earth, and human life. On the other hand, opposed to secular naturalism, biblical theism testifies to the God who is, who is not silent, who spoke us into being, and who reigns over the earth and all His domain.

If we are to persuade a hungering world that our view of reality is true, we must be prepared to advance our case in both word and deed and to present a sound cultural apologetic.

This is a case Christians have made from the earliest days of the church. When Christians were accused of atrocious, heinous crimes against the Roman Empire in the second century, they not only defended Christianity rationally, on the merits of the Christian faith, but also answered the objections of the rulers of Rome by challenging the secular elites to look at the way Christians lived. Justin demonstrated that the Christian life was more rational and created a better ordered society. The writer of the Epistle to Diognetus boasted of the morality of his Christian contemporaries, as did Tertullian a generation later. Augustine engaged in cultural apologetics, famously, of course, in *The City of God,* as did, much later, Aquinas in his sweeping apologetic, *Summa Contra Gentiles.* John Calvin and other reformers carried on this tradition in the Reformation by showing how Christianity improved every sphere of life—personal, communal, and cultural.

We must make precisely this same case today, and we must make it comprehensively, and together. Consider the law that holds the fabric of a nation together. As we have seen, it has been hijacked by judicial activists who say law is not found in any overarching standard but merely in what judges say it is. The public needs to understand that law must be reconnected to transcendent truth, which is precisely what Judeo-Christian revelation provides.

Similarly, a powerful case must be made that Christians have been and are the great defenders of human rights and human dignity, not just for the unborn, but in every area of life. The Star of David and the Cross of Jesus Christ have stood as great scandals to the tyrants of this word because they express belief in a King above the kings of this world. One thinks of the great nineteenth century abolitionist Sojourner Truth; of the English parliamentarian William Wilberforce and the noble effort he led to bring an end to the British slave trade; of Susan B. Anthony, who was a pro-life Quaker. That is our Christian tradition, our common heritage.

Making our cultural apologetic case means we not only argue this, but we demonstrate it. Twenty-five years ago I was unsure of why God called me into prison ministry. There were many other things that I would have preferred to do. I now see why He did. Prison Fellowship is now working in twelve hundred prisons across America, and we're seeing people's lives transformed in an arena where the secular society has simply thrown up its hands in utter despair.

In New York, in 1996, the Center for Social Research conducted a study of the recidivism rate of prisoners who attended Prison Fellowship Bible studies. In their control group of the general population, they found a 41 percent recidivism rate within a short time after being released from prison. If an inmate went to one Bible study, his recidivism rate was 41 percent—exactly the same. But if a prisoner went to ten or more meetings during a year, the recidivism rate dropped to 14 percent—an astonishing 66 percent reduction in recidivism.

We are witnessing exactly the same results in a prison that Prison Fellowship runs in Texas. Two and a half years ago, Gov. George W. Bush gave us permission to do something very radical when he allowed us to take over one program and conduct Christian programming full time. We call the program InnerChange Freedom Initiative, in the Jester II prison just outside of Houston. It's a truly Christian prison modeled on the prisons we've run in South America over the last twenty-five years. The regimen is strict: At 5:30 A.M., the inmates are up for devotions. Then each inmate participates in intense classroom work. After that, some work at jobs, and then all participate in Bible study every evening. The men agree to stay in the program for eighteen months, and some have even turned down parole in order to keep that commitment. Such thorough and extended immersion in the biblical world view changes lives.

Outside of the prisons, we work through a ministry called Angel Tree. Nearly five hundred thousand kids across the country this year, who have a mommy or daddy locked up in prison, will have someone visit them at Christmastime, bring them a gift from their parent in prison, and tell them about Jesus. Patty and I do it every Christmas, and nothing gives me greater joy than going into one of the public housing projects near our home, finding the apartment, and seeing a little kid come out to hear me say, "This is from your daddy," and then seeing his eyes just light up. One year, one little boy said to me, "I knew my daddy wouldn't forget me." Another told me to tell his daddy he really loved him after all. This is now reaching nearly half a million otherwise forgotten kids all across the country. Lives are being transformed; families are being restored.

Understanding and defending Christianity as a comprehensive world view enables us to do something else which, in the long view, may be more important than rescuing a culture. It enables us to achieve Christian unity in a way that could perhaps not be possible otherwise. All Christians must bear the shame of the millennium just ending in which the world has been offended not by the scandal of the Cross, but by the scandal of division among us. Whether it is the division which erupted at the beginning of this millennium between East and West, the rift of the last five hundred years between Roman Catholics and the heirs of the Reformation, or any of the countless rifts and strifes that divide Protestantism today, it is our shame; it belongs to every one of us.

Now, as one who has incurred no small number of battle scars for my stand on Evangelicals and Catholics Together (ECT) and my commitment to reaching out across the confessional divides, I want to be the first to say that there are yet deep and profound divisions which remain between communions. We have made some progress in the ongoing dialogue called Evangelicals and Catholics Together, but I do not minimize or trivialize the issues that separate us. But the fact is, as we begin to see Christianity as a world view, we are able to do what Cardinal Cassidy argued is the duty of Christians: to work for unity, because unity is the normative condition that Jesus Himself called for and established. It is unity for which Jesus prayed, and to work against it is a sin. Seeing our faith as a world view helps us to work toward that divinely sanctioned condition, because, while divisions remain among us, we nevertheless engage in what my good friend, Dr. Timothy George of Beeson Divinity School, calls "the ecumenism of the trenches." We discover that we stand and fight side by side as Evangelicals and Roman Catholics. In doing so, we are enabled to see beyond those divisions, as important as they are, when our focus is upon the great contours of Christian truth as it is presented and defended in the world.

There was no more determined a Calvinist reformer than Abraham Kuyper, the great Dutch theologian and political leader of a century ago. He saw clearly our need for unity. In his famous "Stone Lectures" of 1898 at Princeton, Kuyper described what happens when we see Christianity as a world view: We "might be enabled once more to take our stand by the side of Romanism in opposition to modern pantheism. For what we have in common with Rome are precisely those fundamentals of our Christian creed now most fiercely assaulted by the modern spirit. If Roman Catholics pick up the sword and do valiant and skillful battle against the same enemy," Kuyper argued, "is it not the part of wisdom to accept their valuable help?" It is precisely this kind of ecumenism of the trenches that moved Father Neuhaus and me to begin the work of ECT.

Now the spirit of ECT is spreading around the world. A group similar to ours has been meeting for several years in the Republic of Ireland. Just recently, I received an invitation to speak to a group of churches in Nebraska. This group of churches—several Protestant churches of various denominations and a number of Roman Catholic churches—had been meeting together to discuss how to put ECT into practice. In South America, Evangelical leaders have been meeting with the Catholic Bishops' Conference, and just recently issued their first joint statement. And just a few weeks ago, in Sofia, Bulgaria, the ministries of Prison Fellowship International came together for our international convocation. On the closing night, the host ministry, which is heavily influenced by the Bulgarian Orthodox Church, held the communion service. Unconsecrated bread was shared by Protestant,

Catholic, and Orthodox believers in a spirit celebrating the great truths held in common in Christ.

I believe we can succeed in bringing Christian truth to bear on our culture and begin to see a springtime of evangelization only if we stand together in defense of our common faith, drawing upon the best of our respective traditions. The Roman Catholic tradition offers much: the church's historic role in the culture, the authority of the magisterium, the commitment to scholarship, and the long tradition of reflection on social and political issues, particularly the concern for social justice and the poor. As an Evangelical, I have to confess that the Roman Catholics were in the trenches of warfare in the pro-life movement before we were. We were laggards until Francis Schaeffer challenged us in the seventies. The Catholic tradition brings a great commitment to the life of the mind, as well as a passion for the arts. It is a tradition with an appreciation of a well-formed world view.

On the Evangelical side, we bring much to the table as well, especially what I call the Evangelical impulse. The Evangelical impulse is fueled by three distinct elements of Evangelicalism: First, an emphasis on personal conversion; second, the devotion to Scripture; and third, belief in the priesthood of all believers.

First, conversion—for which I am Exhibit A. Twenty-six years ago, in the darkest days of Watergate, I was at best a nominal Christian who went to church twice a year, at Easter and Christmas. Having heard the words of C. S. Lewis read to me in the darkest days of Watergate, I found myself, the toughest of the Nixon tough guys, ex-marine captain, and White House hatchet man, in a flood of tears in an automobile, crying so hard I couldn't pull out of my friend's driveway. For the first time, I had heard the gospel. Even after all these years, I still think of that moment with the deepest joy and emotion. I can never forget what it felt like to know that my sins had been taken away because

Jesus Christ went to the Cross and died that I might be saved. Every day when I get up, I thank God for that moment in my life. It compels me to do what I do, because, as Chesterton wrote, "Gratitude is the mother of all virtues." I'm so grateful to God for what He's done in my life that I have no choice but to do my duty as He calls. I will never get over that moment, and if it weren't for my conversion, I know that I would have suffocated in the stench of my own sin.

I BELIEVE WE CAN. . .
BEGIN TO SEE A SPRINGTIME
OF EVANGELIZATION ONLY IF
WE STAND TOGETHER IN DEFENSE
OF OUR COMMON FAITH,
DRAWING UPON THE BEST OF
OUR RESPECTIVE TRADITIONS.

The second element in the Evangelical impulse is devotion to Scripture. Many years ago now, I received a letter from the pastor of one of the largest mainline churches in New York who had been sending twenty-five or thirty dollars a month as a contribution to Prison Fellowship. He wrote to say that he loved what I was doing in prisons, but he questioned whether he could continue to support me because of my belief in the inerrancy of Scripture. I replied to his letter by explaining that I do what I do precisely because the Scriptures command me to do so. If I questioned the truth or authority of Scripture, I would not do it. "So," I wrote to him, "the thing you don't like about me is the thing that causes me to do what you do like." The next month he sent double his normal contribution. It is this passionate belief in the authority and inerrancy of Scripture that moves so many hundreds of thousands of Evangelicals to works of Christian service.

The third element of the Evangelical impulse is the priesthood of all believers. This is one of the great legacies of the Reformation because it broke the secular-sacred divide. In the Reformed view, all work is done for the glory of God, all work is a calling, and all people, clergy and laity alike, are to be involved in holy works of service. Luther liked to quote Erasmus, "The farm boy at the plow and the milkmaid at the pail have the Word of God in their hands and read it with their eyes."

That is what energizes a whole army of people to do marvelous works of service, turning every legitimate vocation into a ministry.

The Evangelical impulse played a key role not only in the Reformation but thereafter through the eighteenth and nineteenth centuries, and even into the twentieth century. The Reformers' high view of work—vocation being the path of discipleship—fueled the work ethic that so profoundly affected this country. It burst forth in the Great Awakening when George Whitefield preached throughout the colonies, resulting in a series of powerful renewals.

The Second Great Awakening in this country saw eleven hundred social reform organizations organized to combat poverty, drunkenness (even dueling), and to initiate important poorhouse reforms. Over six hundred colleges and universities were founded as a result of this great moving of God's Spirit.

A similar effect occurred in England. John Wesley said there could be no holiness without social justice and led a movement that transformed his country. Under the leadership of Wesley's disciple, William Wilberforce, victory over the practice of slavery in England was achieved. For twenty years, Wilberforce led a persistent movement until, in 1807, the English parliament abolished the slave trade. Their efforts were carried on by Shaftesbury and other reformers of the Victorian era, resulting in the release of fourteen thousand people who'd been languishing in debtor's prison, the reform of child labor abuses, the building of public hospitals, the reform of the prisons, and the wonderful work that was carried on by Elizabeth Fry and John Howard.

Those who say today that we should give up on the culture—that there's nothing more we can do to win the culture war—should study the history of the great revival that began in 1858, when just ten men gathered to pray in downtown New York in the Dutch Reformed Old North Church. They assembled under the gathering storm clouds of war, in a time of great economic uncertainty. Jeremiah Lanphier gathered ten men to pray every day at noon. Before long, seven hundred churches joined them. Within six months, every public facility in New York City was filled to overflowing, and ten thousand people were in the streets gathering every day for prayer at noon.

That revival spread up the Hudson River, into Canada, across the sea to England, throughout Europe, and then on to the entire English-speaking world. It resulted in the Great Awakening of the latter half of the nineteenth century, out of which came such organizations as The Salvation Army, a pure demonstration of Evangelical enthusiasm. In this country, it inspired the great work that followed from the preaching of Dwight Moody, whose social contributions many have underestimated. It is ironic that some of Moody's spiritual heirs are critical of the work of ECT. If Moody were alive today, he would be one of the first at the ECT table. In 1893 Moody invited Roman Catholics to the platform at his crusade in Chicago. More significantly, in his hometown of Northfield, Massachusetts, Moody contributed to the building of a Roman Catholic church, arguing that if people are going to be Christians, whether they're Catholic or Protestant, the object is to help them to be good Christians.

Though less well known, one of the great expressions of the Evangelical impulse was in 1904. It began in Wales, with the preaching of Evan Roberts. It started in one Evangelical church and spread throughout the churches of Wales. There were, within five months, one hundred thousand converts. The effect on culture was profound. J. Edwin Orr, the great historian of revivals, reports that the revival had such an effect upon Wales that after the 1905 New Year, the Swansea County Police Court announced that there had not been a single charge of drunkenness on the holiday weekend for the first time in recorded history. A great wave of sobriety swept over the country. Many of the taverns were closed. Bookstores could not keep Bibles on the shelves. Gamblers were converted, stolen goods returned, court calendars cleared, and the police were so panicked over the fear they would become unemployed that district councils were called into emergency session. It even affected commerce, but in a surprising way. So many men gave up their foul language that the pit ponies in the mines, which dragged the coal trucks for mine companies, did not understand what was being said to them and, for a time, couldn't follow directions.

I believe in the very depth of my being that if Catholics and Evangelicals come together, drawing on the great strengths of our two traditions; if God so chooses and fuels us with this Evangelical impulse, this love of God which comes from our conversion; and if we are faithful to obey the scriptural commandments, a great army of people will be unleashed to defend and demonstrate Christian truth in the world. This can indeed then usher in a great springtime of Evangelization.

Ours is a truly wonderful opportunity as the world looks around and surveys the shambles of the modern experiment.

The history of the twentieth century is a catalogue of failed "-isms"—all of the great utopian promises. It started with post-

Edwardian triumphalism, wonderfully captured in the movie *Titanic*. In the film, there's a marvelous scene when a British aristocrat starts to board the ship. He looks up at it, this enormous feat of modern engineering, and he arrogantly proclaims, "Even God couldn't sink this ship." You know the rest.

> OURS IS A TRULY WONDERFUL OPPORTUNITY AS THE WORLD LOOKS AROUND AND SURVEYS THE SHAMBLES OF THE MODERN EXPERIMENT.

The same fate has befallen every one of the other twentieth century "-isms": Darwin's and Hegel's ideas about continuing revolution and progress; the utopianism of Dewey and Freud that has crippled education and our sense of responsibility; scientism; Marxism; national socialism; humanism; materialism; consumerism. All of the great utopian promises of the twentieth century lie in shambles. Some of them are still with us today, but they're bankrupt ideas waiting to be swept onto the dust heap of history. We stand at a moment in time—a remarkable, extraordinary moment—when, if, following the examples of Erasmus and Kuyper and the teaching of Jesus, Christians can come together across those historic divides and bring the great strengths of our traditions to bear, together holding out to the world a promise of a better and more rational way to organize their lives, we will see that springtime of evangelism come to glorious harvest.

Five Characteristics
of Christian Leadership

Prison Fellowship International Convocation
Arlington, Virginia
August, 1995

When I think of leadership, I sometimes think of George. George is twenty-eight years old. He is single and still lives at home with his parents. One Sunday morning George just couldn't bring himself to get up. The alarm went off, and he hit the button to stop the noise.

Twenty minutes later his mother knocked at the door. "George, George, you must get up. It is Sunday morning, and you will be late for church."

George said, "Mother, I am not going to church. Three reasons: one, I am tired; two, the people there don't like me; three, the sermons are dull."

His mother said, "George, you are going to church, and for these three reasons: first, it is Sunday, and we always worship on Sunday; second, it doesn't matter whether they like us or not; third, you are the pastor!"

When it comes to leadership, I suspect we are all like George sometimes. Leadership is something that we would just as soon not assume because it is painful. You have to step out of the crowd.

I can identify with that. Lots of times, before I pack my suitcases to go on a trip, I think, *I just can't do this.* I can't quite get myself up to do it. Maybe that is not so bad, because leadership is something that we don't choose for ourselves or even seek or desire; rather, it is something to which we are called.

Let me preface this presentation with something quite appropriate that Tom Pratt, president of Prison Fellowship Ministries in the U.S.A., said to me recently: "If you want to know about leadership, don't read books about leadership; read books about leaders." Study leaders themselves.

The world studies about leaders like Churchill or Alexander the Great, Julius Caesar, Franklin Roosevelt, General MacArthur, Montgomery, or Napoleon. But the Christian has the greatest roster of leaders to learn from, their stories being told in the Scriptures. And for a Christian leader, Scripture gives an example in every category of leadership.

Call to Leadership

Let's start at the beginning, with being called to leadership. Have you ever noticed that not one biblical leader wanted the job? Okay, maybe Isaiah. Isaiah got burned on the lips with a hot coal, and that would make most anybody say, "Lord, I will do anything You want me to do!" But Moses—he said he couldn't speak. So the Lord gave him a mouthpiece. That was the first lawyer, you might say. Solomon felt he was too young. David and all of the prophets shirked from the role. Jonah! The title of a new film about me, *The Reluctant Prophet,* indicates how I identify with Jonah. I did not want to start a Christian ministry to prisoners. God did not have to throw me into the belly of the whale, but He threw me in prison and prepared me for the call on my life.

The first thing we recognize about Christian leadership is that a leader is called, is sent. Here's an example: "The LORD said to Moses, 'Send some men to explore the land of Canaan which I am giving to the Israelites. From each ancestral tribe send one of its leaders.' So at the LORD's command, Moses sent them out from the Desert of Paran. All of them were leaders of the Israelites" (Num. 13:1–3 NIV). All through the Scriptures, you see that the biblical leader is one who is called, usually reluctant and not wanting the role, but one who is sent. So the first sign of Christian leadership is calling—the fact that you are called.

FOR A CHRISTIAN LEADER, SCRIPTURE GIVES AN EXAMPLE IN EVERY CATEGORY OF LEADERSHIP.

A little book called *Spiritual Leadership* was written by Oswald Sanders, a New Zealander. It has been in print now for perhaps forty years, and it lays out principles of spiritual leadership like nothing else that I have read; as a matter of fact, we give it to all new directors in Prison Fellowship U.S.A. with the requirement that they read it. Sanders quotes Dr. A. W. Tozer, who says this about calling:

> *A true and safe leader is likely to be one who has no desire to lead, but is forced into a position of leadership by the inward pressure of the Holy Spirit and the press of external situations, such as Moses and David and the Old Testament prophets. I think there was hardly a great leader from Paul*

to the present day but was drafted by the Holy Spirit for the task and commissioned by the Lord of the church to fill a position that he, the individual, had little heart for. I believe it might be accepted as a fairly reliable rule of thumb that the man who is ambitious to lead is disqualified as a leader.

Plato once said something very wise. He said, "He who seeks power is not fit to hold it." The desire for building up ourselves is totally contrary to all the principles of Christian leadership. The whole object of Christian leadership is to fulfill a call that God puts upon your life, and most often you are going to be reluctant because a great deal of pain goes with that. If you begin to think, "Ah! I like this job of being a Christian leader," watch out! The leader who is in it because it gratifies his ego is doomed.

Two comments: Over the years, I have heard people refer to "my ministry." As they say "my ministry" this and "my ministry" that, I know that person is in trouble. I think about a very prominent person, whose name you might well know, who kept talking about "my ministry" as if God had given him this to be "his"; that man fell terribly; he was ruined, lost. No, the leader should never be personally ambitious.

You should enjoy leadership because you are being fulfilled and used by God, but you should not enjoy it because it fulfills your own ego needs. If you begin to feel that it is you, yourself, that is being built up, you need to run away from it, though it is difficult to know that about oneself.

Which brings me to my second comment: It is critical to understand that you are probably the worst judge of your motives. If you really want to know if you are called and fulfilling God's will, you had better have a few people you really trust to whom you can hold yourself accountable. In my book *The Body*, I talk about the necessity of a small accountability group. I have a few members of the Prison Fellowship board of directors whom I call and say, "Is this right? Are my instincts correct?" If I don't get a unanimous reaction from these men, I don't act, because the Holy Spirit will not speak with a forked tongue. The Holy Spirit will tell all of my brothers exactly the same thing. When there is unanimity, I know the Holy Spirit is speaking, and I know that there is a check upon me.

The first requirement, therefore, of leadership is the sense of calling and the realization that this is what God has made you do; you can't do anything else but follow. I wrestled with God for a year before I went into prison ministry. Literally so, because I really didn't want it. Once I was sure that this was what God wanted for my life, at that point I surrendered and said yes. That wrestling period was an important period for me, because it was a way for me to check out that this was not something that I was doing for Chuck Colson but rather something I believed I was doing at God's call and upon His insistence.

Number one: You are called, and you know it is God's call on your life. You can't turn away from it; you have no choice. You have tried to get away from it, and you can't. It is God's call on your life. You may not like it; you may not want it. You ought to be reluctant; you ought to be frightened of the role; but once you are called, you go do it.

God-Directed Vision

Number two: Then you work to cultivate God's perspective—the divine perspective on the task that God has given you. It will be the first charisma you will get, the first gift of God—the ability to see in a divine perspective.

So the second primary characteristic of the Christian leader is seeing the world not in one's own perspective, but rather in God's perspective. In other words, you have a God-directed vision of what you are supposed to do.

This is one of my favorite stories in all of Scripture: The king of Aram, at war with Israel, was moving his armies around. Someone kept getting word to the Israelites, so they knew where he was going to set up camp. The enraged king summoned his officers, and he said, "Tell me which one of you is on the side of the king of Israel?" Eventually he realized it was the prophet Elisha. With that information, the king said: "Go, find out where he is so I can send men and capture him." The report came back: "He is in Dothan." So the king sent horses and chariots and soldiers to Dothan. By night they surrounded the city. When Elisha's servant got up and went out early the next morning, an army with horses and chariots had surrounded the city. "Oh, my lord, what shall we do?" I mean, they were surrounded! Hopeless! The Israelites had been caught and trapped by a heathen army. Elisha said this: "Do not be afraid, those who are with us are more than those who are with them."

What did Elisha see? Elisha saw chariots of fire and God's army, and it outnumbered the army of the king of Aram. But only Elisha could see the forces; his servant couldn't. Then Elisha prayed, "O LORD, open his eyes so he may see."

"The LORD opened the servant's eyes, and he looked and saw the hills full of horses and chariots of fire all around Elisha" (see 2 Kings 6:13–17 NIV).

You may know the rest of the story. Elisha was victorious. What is the lesson here? In the context of every human relationship, human nature is such that we don't see beyond our own narrow horizon.

It is the job of a Christian leader to say, "Those who are with us are greater than those who are against us." To see God's chariots of fire. To see God's purpose for the ultimate victory of His people. To inspire those who are filled with fear, crying, "What shall we do?" by saying, "Don't worry. Those with us are greater than those against us." The leader sees something the follower cannot see.

As leaders in the church of Jesus Christ—if you are indeed leaders—you are seeing something the people in that church don't see. People in that church sit there comfortably Sunday after Sunday having their ears tickled and being unwilling to move from one place to the next. People don't like to move.

IT IS THE JOB OF A CHRISTIAN LEADER TO SAY, "THOSE WHO ARE WITH US ARE GREATER THAN THOSE WHO ARE AGAINST US."

As a young man, I served in the United States Marine Corps. I went into the marines at the time of the Korean War. I went through training camp as a young lieutenant at a time when 50 percent of the lieutenants were coming back from Korea in pine boxes—casualties. I remember being told in basic training that my job was to stand up in the middle of combat and say, "Follow me." And, of course, the fellow who stands up gets shot! But that is your job. You stand up and say, "Follow me," because everybody else wants to stay in his trench.

It is the problem with the church today that members want to stay in their own comfort zones; this means that somebody has to stand up and say, "Those who are with us are more than those who are against us. I see things with God's perspective. Come on, follow me." And remember, too, that biblical principle: Jesus never says to go do anything that He hasn't done first. What did He say in

Mark 1:17? "Follow me, and I will make you fishers of men." He is not saying "you have to take this," but that He will not leave us. He leads the way and simply calls us to follow.

It is not easy. It is not popular. It is one reason that anybody who thinks seriously about Christian service has an instant reaction to flee from it because it is great pain. But the visionary is one who always lifts people above their own self-interest. People naturally see the world through their own lens, through their own filter of self-interest. The job of the leader is to enable people to see something greater than themselves and call them to do it.

Godly Character

The third characteristic of godly leadership is that you must have the character—the godly character—by which you have the authority to call other people to do that which they basically don't want to do. People generally do not want to minister in prisons. When you ask people to do so, you are seeing something they are not seeing. You are seeing things from a divine perspective that says we are to go and care for the prisoner. You call people to do something they don't want to do. But they are not going to follow you in ministry unless you have a godly character that they will respect and that gives you the authority to exercise that leadership.

Speaking of my service in the marines. . . Not long ago I addressed all of the officers and noncommissioned officers of the Second Marine Division at Camp Lejeune, North Carolina. As you may know, the creed of the U.S. Marine Corps is *semper fidelis*—always faithful, always following orders. The U.S. Marine Corps is the most disciplined military organization in America, perhaps in the world.

After I spoke for forty minutes on ethics, a noncommissioned officer, an African American, stood up and said, "Mr. Colson, let me ask you a question. Which is the greater quality, 'loyalty' or 'integrity'?" What a wonderful question! Probably twenty years ago that would not have been asked in a military organization, at least not in America. Loyalty meant simply doing what your officer commanded you to do. But this man stood there wrestling with the most critical question. Military organizations and every other organization have to ask it. Of course, the answer is easy, even to those who live by the creed of *semper fidelis*. The answer is integrity, because without integrity, loyalty can mislead you. Integrity means wholeness. It means that we are who we say we are, that as Christians we walk our talk; as Christians we behave the way we say we believe. Our beliefs are put into practice in our lives.

We may be flawed. We may have lots of sins. There are a lot of things God is dealing with in my life, and He has to deal with them constantly. That is why the apostle Paul said, "I die every day" (see 1 Cor. 15:31), because he had a problem that he had to deal with every single day. So do I. If you don't, you probably will lie about other things as well! We all have problems. But our job as leaders is to be every day coming closer to conforming to the image of Christ, to be more Christlike in the way we live.

As Christ begins to fill us up, we begin to draw the moral authority with which we can lead. It doesn't mean that we are to be wimps or weaklings. If God has called you, you have a certain authority that goes with that. And yet you are not "authoritarian." I hope you will think about those two words—authority and authoritarian—because there is a powerful difference between them. I have watched pastors get up to preach; having traveled all over the world and in twenty years of ministry having met all the great names—I can tell if a preacher is authoritarian when he gets up to talk by the way he walks, the way he conducts himself, the way he says "God" (with an extra syllable), and the way in which he exerts his authority.

I think the best example of someone having authority without being authoritarian is Mother Teresa: ninety pounds, meek, hunched over, physically weak so she had to be helped from place to place. But she came to Washington and spoke at the National Prayer Breakfast and stood at that podium and spoke with moral authority and power. Extraordinary! God simply came down and spoke through her because of her own godliness. You can have great authority without being authoritarian, because your authority comes not from yourself or from your manner or your demeanor, but from your righteousness and your holy living and the fact that God is working through you.

There's no excuse to be sloppy. No excuse simply to say, "God is going to work through me." I think of General Eisenhower when he was making the decision about landing at D-Day. It was a terribly hard decision—terrible! He was surrounded by all of his generals, and General Montgomery was telling him not to land; another general was telling him that he should land. And he was listening to the weather forecast. All the time General Eisenhower never said a word. He paced back and forth listening. Never showed weakness. He must have been nervous. He must have been scared to death. The fate of the war was in his hands. The success of the armies that were arrayed against Hitler was in his hands. Maybe the fate of the West was in his hands at that point. Maybe the fate of the world! And he was listening to conflicting advice from two groups.

I heard a talk by a man who was there and watched him that day. General Eisenhower never said a word. He just listened and listened. And then, finally, he said, "All right, I have made a decision. Here is what we will do." He couldn't have been sure that he was right at that moment, but he could not convey weakness to the people who were following him because he had the authority at that point. You cannot convey weakness, but at the same time you can never be authoritarian, that is, attempting to lord what you have over other people.

The leader serves. A biblical story that has come to have great meaning to me in recent months is of David, when he was battling with the Philistines (see 1 Chron. 11:15–19). The Philistines outnumbered and surrounded David, whose fortress was the cave of Adullam. It was hot in Palestine; the weather was grueling, and he was thirsty and tired. David said, "Oh, that someone would get me a drink of water from the well near the gate of Bethlehem!"—his hometown.

Three of his soldiers overheard him. Three mighty men got up and broke through the Philistine lines, drew water from the Bethlehem well, and carried it back to David. At that moment they might have thought that they had made a great sacrifice for their leader, their general, the man who was defending Israel, who was charging against the enemy lines.

They brought him the water he wanted so badly. But he refused to drink it. Instead he took the water, and he dumped it out on the ground. Can you imagine what those men thought? Those men had to think, *I just risked my life to get my leader a drink of water, which he had wished for, and he poured it out on the ground!* I mean, they would be exasperated. He refused to drink it. Instead he poured it out with these critical words before the Lord: "Far be it from me, O Lord, to do this," he said. "Is it not the blood of men who went at the risk of their lives?" You see what David was saying to those men? *Yes, I want that water. My lips are parched. My throat is dry. I want that water badly, but I am not going to take it at the expense of your life.*

There is a long military tradition, and I discovered this is true in all countries around the world: When the officer takes his troops into the field, the officer is always certain that his troops are fed first. It follows from this biblical story, when David said, "I want that water, but even more I want you to know that I respect you, and therefore only the Lord is worthy of this sacrifice, so we pour this water out before the Lord."

We pour ourselves out for those whom we serve. We do so with the authority that God has given us to lead, by being utterly humble. Doesn't the Scripture tell us that no man before or later was more humble than Moses who had to lead six hundred thousand rebellious people through the desert for forty years? The application is that we serve our God and not ourselves and never abuse our leadership in service to ourselves. Our followers then understand that it is God's authority that enables us to lead them.

WE POUR OURSELVES OUT FOR THOSE WHOM WE SERVE.

Security to Build Up Others

The fourth characteristic of Christian leadership is to build or raise up others, always. When you have authority, it is very tempting to draw it into yourself. The insecure leader is always looking for more authority and is always fearful that other people will take away his authority. A Christian leader should be utterly secure, knowing that God has given the authority to—invested it in—him or her. Know that it is God's authority, that He can take it away tomorrow, and that the task, particularly in a movement like Prison Fellowship, is to raise up other people.

I think of what happened with Moses in regard to Eldad and Medad. They were listed among the "seventy elders," but they didn't go with other leaders to the "Tent of Meeting" with Moses, where God was going to "put the Spirit" on the elders. Even so, the Spirit rested on these two, and they prophesied back "in the camp." Here was Moses, the leader, and two of his deacons prophesying outside the official "tent." Immediately Joshua, one of the strongest of Moses' lieutenants, said, "Moses! Stop them! What are they doing taking over your responsibilities?" In organizations have you ever had people come to you and say, "That subordinate is trying to take your job away"? That is exactly what Joshua said to Moses. Listen to Moses' answer: "Are you jealous for my sake? I wish that all the LORD'S people were prophets and that the LORD would put his Spirit on them" (see Num. 11:16–30 NIV).

The true mark of a Christian leader is trying to build up other people. Raise up other leaders! The strength of your movement depends on the strength of the people whom you raise, teach, disciple, lead, and to whom you pass on the vision that they might carry on the ministry. Don't hog it to yourself.

Godly Perseverance

The fifth characteristic of the Christian leader, in my view, is what I call godly perseverance. It is not enough to say, "This is what we are going to go do," because human nature is rebellious. Human nature is stubborn. Every time I get discouraged in anything I am doing in Prison Fellowship, I usually go back and I read a little bit more about the life of Moses.

Can you imagine anybody with a tougher job? I mean, here he is—he is eighty years old and confronts God in the burning bush. He doesn't want this. He can't speak. He is being told that he is going to go back to Pharaoh and say, "Set my people free," and he is thinking, *Are You kidding?* And then he gets them free, and what do they do? They turn on him at every opportunity. Eventually Moses lost it. After all those years, he lost it (that is what cost him his leadership), when he struck the rock at Meribah to bring the water out himself rather than to trust God to bring it forth for him. But before that— what he put up with all those years—that is absolutely amazing.

What the apostle Paul put up with all of those years proclaiming the gospel, being beaten, stoned, imprisoned, dragged out of the city, kicked, whipped, spit upon! Yet never did he stop proclaiming the wonderful, saving truth of Jesus Christ. No! Godly perseverance takes enormous courage.

This year I signed a document called "Evangelicals and Catholics Together," because I feel so passionately that orthodox, Bible-believing Christians must stand together as our witness to the world and in defense of Christian truth. But it has caused enormous controversy. And there were times, I must tell you, when I thought, *Have I made a mistake? Am I into more controversy than I really wanted? Have I injured the ministry of Prison Fellowship?* There have been some times when I have had grave doubts, and yet I kept feeling a conviction of the Holy Spirit that what I was doing was God's calling. Again, I didn't want to do it. It wasn't something I wanted. But I felt called that I must do it and must persevere.

A few times I checked with my brothers who hold me account-able. *Am I all right? Am I going too far?* But even at those times when I wanted to flee, I could not flee. Martin Luther, when he stood before the authorities of the day, said, "My conscience holds me captive. I cannot recant." He later said his knees were trembling when he said that.

Christian leadership takes enormous courage, perseverance, and steadfastness. You must stay with it. The world will mock. Believe me! The more Christian you are, the more you are subject to the ridicule and mockery of the world, and the more you must persevere, and persevere with courage.

Courage is not rashness. The best illustration of courage was given by Aristotle in what he calls the "golden mean." This is often misinterpreted, because people think that means finding the comfortable middle. Not at all! Aristotle said all human emotions cover a range from one extreme to another. On one extreme is rashness. On the other extreme is cowardice. The "golden mean" is courage. Don't go too far over to one side, or you are rash and irresponsible. Don't go too far over the other way, or you are a coward. But find that golden mean in human emotion that gives you the courage to persevere. And you can find it only on your knees.

> THE MORE CHRISTIAN YOU ARE, THE MORE YOU ARE SUBJECT TO THE RIDICULE AND MOCKERY OF THE WORLD, AND THE MORE YOU MUST PERSEVERE, AND PERSEVERE WITH COURAGE.

Guarding the Trust

Finally, although I would not call it a characteristic of Christian leadership, I note that the Christian leader always has to be aware of the holy trust given in a leadership role. You mess up, and you bring stain to the name of Christ! Don't you dare!

If you are not filled with holy terror, you should not be in ministry. You need these qualities of being called, of having the vision, of having holy perseverance, godly perseverance, of having the godly character that goes with it, and of having the courage that is also part of that holy perseverance. But in the final analysis, never, never, never forget that it is a holy trust that you have been given. Spiritual means can be achieved only by spiritual people with spiritual goals.

That is laid out so beautifully in Oswald Sanders's book *Spiritual*

Leadership. That book and, more importantly, the Bible will drive you to your knees if you realize that God has called you and given you this holy trust. Martin Luther, tough fellow, stood against the church and the state. He said he never once got up to preach that his knees did not knock. Charles Haddon Spurgeon, probably the greatest preacher of the nineteenth century, had twelve thousand books in his library. Before he died, he had read every single one of them! If you have ever read any of Spurgeon's sermons, you will see an extraordinary mind and biblical knowledge. Spurgeon said that to preach the whole counsel of God is an awful charge. Elisha, when he was coming to take the mantle from Elijah, was terrified. "Give me a double portion of the spirit you have" (see 2 Kings 2:9).

I have never yet in twenty years of Christian ministry, all over the world, gotten up to speak without being frightened. Not frightened that I won't be able to speak, because I know I can speak as I did it in politics. No, rather I'm frightened that I might in some way betray the holy trust God has given me.

Above all else, above all qualities of leadership, remember the sacredness of the calling that God has given you to lead and to be His witnesses in the world.

Comments on Commencing Ministry

Gordon-Conwell Theological Seminary
South Hamilton, Massachusetts
Commencement, 1999

Graduations are wonderful occasions, churning up many mixed feelings. A seminary commencement marks a beginning—you're being launched into the work of Christian ministry. As graduates, you feel pride in achievement. You feel jubilation.

There is a sense of relief; no more study. But don't kid yourself. Your formal education here is just the beginning of your study. A pivotal moment in my Christian life was when, in 1977, I met Prof. Richard Lovelace (of Gordon-Conwell) to whom I owe a great debt. He helped me discover that if I was going to be a Christian and in any kind of position of leadership, I needed to study. He introduced me to the field of church history. I didn't have the advantage of going through a theological institution and studying with a magnificent faculty as you have. But at the feet of Richard Lovelace, I developed an intellectual hunger, a thirst for knowledge to know more about God and His work in the world, and then theology. I trust you will discover that ministry continually challenges the mind to make you think Christianly about all of life.

Our Holy Trust

Graduations also bring—or should bring—a sense of humility as you leave here knowing that God is giving you a holy trust. That is what ministry is. I remember being commissioned as an officer in the Marine Corps in the Korean War era. I felt great honor in putting the bars on my shoulder and that Marine Corps globe and anchor on my lapel. But I also was apprehensive. As a twenty-one-year-old, though I couldn't show it, I felt terrified realizing that I would have the lives of fifty men in my hands. They would depend on me to stay alive. As a Christian and minister of the gospel, you have a similar charge. But think how much more is entrusted to you: the eternal destiny of the people you will come in contact with. There cannot be any more sacred, humbling trust for any human being than to go forth and say, "I am a Christian." This is true for all of us, not just those in the ministry, but it is a special burden to you. You are constantly on duty.

I remember one particular day some years ago, standing in line at the Jakarta airport. I was very tired. I had flown all night, and then I got held up in immigration. We had a very busy schedule that day. People who were supposed to have escorted us through customs didn't. To make a long story short, I was feeling very frustrated, standing there in line for a half an hour. . . .

Well, two years later I received a letter from a lawyer of Chinese descent in Singapore. "Dear Mr. Colson," he wrote, "I grew up in the superstitions of the Chinese people. I had no interest in Christianity, but I sent my son and daughter to a Sunday school because I wanted them to learn some moral teachings." He continued: "A missionary came to the church one day when I was delivering the kids. He held up your book, *Born Again*, and said something about you. I was fascinated by that, and I went and got the book. I didn't read it, but the cover was on my table at home." This is the interesting part: "Two years ago (you wouldn't remember this), I was standing in the immigration line in Jakarta, and I looked over and saw your profile, which was on the book. I watched you for the next half hour. I was tired and frustrated and angry, but you weren't." (If he only had known!) "I went home; I got that book; I read it; and at the end, in tears, I gave my life to Christ."

> THERE CANNOT BE
> ANY MORE SACRED,
> HUMBLING TRUST FOR
> ANY HUMAN BEING
> THAN TO GO FORTH AND SAY,
> "I AM A CHRISTIAN."

You never know! You never know how God will use. . .a casual, positive word, a smile to someone who is discouraged, a helping hand to somebody who needs it, an act of faithfulness to what you say you believe, a determination not to let the carnal self get the better of you. You may never know how God will use that! But what a holy and awesome trust we have as Christians being called to walk humbly with God, trusting Him as our strength for ministry—all Christians, but especially those in leadership.

It has always been that way. Moses didn't feel adequate for the job he was given. Because Moses couldn't speak, God had to appoint a mouthpiece—the first lawyer, you might say (and a sign of God's curse). Jeremiah didn't know how to speak, and God touched his lips. I never speak to an audience before asking God to touch my lips as he touched Jeremiah's. Solomon said he was too young to be king.

God gave him wisdom never given to anyone before or since. Paul, for all of his pride, said that he was filled with fear and trembling. Martin Luther, who stood against the entire empire and the church, nonetheless said that whenever he preached, his knees knocked. Augustine claimed he was never satisfied with his preaching: "My preaching always displeased me." Charles Haddon Spurgeon was a man with twelve thousand books in his library. (A visitor once noted that Spurgeon could go to any one of those books and tell him what was in it. An incredible mind!) Spurgeon's London sermons were reprinted every week and distributed all over the world. Spurgeon said this: "We tremble lest we should mistake or misunderstand the Word." To preach the whole truth is a weighty charge!

In ministry, if you ever think that you have got it "figured out," that you are in control, that you aren't dependent on a holy God, that you aren't awed by the trust He has given you—hang it up. I would quit tomorrow if I thought that way. I would stop preaching. I would close my ministry.

But filled with that holy fear, filled with that awe that fills you with a deep sense of humility, go forward and boldly proclaim the truth, which you know. Preach truth to a generation that knows no truth. Preach historic revelation to a generation that says that history is nothing but a social construction. Preach commitment to a generation that rejects all commitment. Preach salvation to a generation that doesn't know that it has anything it needs to be saved from. A tough charge! Challenging, but thrilling! Thrilling because of the times we live in.

Our Comfortable Temptation

Just think about the current opportunity before all of us as Christians. We are about to mark two thousand years of human history, our very calendars dating from the birth of Jesus the Savior.

All of our civilization is impacted by Christian truth handed down through the centuries, and we are celebrating two thousand years. Yet there are Christians among us saying, "Give up on the culture. Don't worry about it. Just go build up our churches." It is a comfortable message, but it is dead wrong, because this ought to be the time when we as jubilant Christians proclaim Truth to the world because the world is hungering to hear it.

Why is it wrong for us to withdraw? It is tempting, of course. It happened to the church earlier in the century. We withdrew; we built our own churches. As pastors you will be under great pressure to recruit and build your churches and make them seeker-sensitive and "bring people in." All of that is wonderful, but never forget that the whole world has been given to us by God. We need to think of the entire world, not just of our own churches and filling our own pews.

No. Withdrawing from the world is wrong for three reasons:

First, I sense that the desire to withdraw is rooted in despair. People are saying, "Let's give up. So many of the battles in the cultural wars have failed; Christian moralistic crusades have failed." But I say, "No. Do not give up, because despair is a sin; it is a sin because it denies the sovereignty of God." We live in constant eschatological expectation—for the return of the King. And we know He will return.

Second, it is a mistake to withdraw, because biblically we are told that the entire world is the Lord's. Consider Psalm 8, among others. "O LORD, our LORD, how majestic is your name in all the earth." When Abraham Kuyper dedicated the Free University in Holland, he said: "There is not one square inch in the whole domain of our human existence over which Christ, who is sovereign over all, does not cry out, 'Mine!'" It is all God's! All learning, all science, every discipline, every area of knowledge—it is God's! We are called to take dominion over it, to be fruitful and increase and subdue it, and to rule over the fish and the birds of the air and every living creature that moves on the ground. We aren't just to be concerned with ourselves. We are concerned with the entire world.

Third, to run away now from the battle of bringing Christian truth to bear on our culture would be to sound the defeat at the very time when victory is within our grasp. Things are changing. There is good news to report. Look at all the cultural indicators. The crime rate is down to pre-1973 levels. There are a lot of reasons for that, including demographics, but there has been a precipitous drop in the last five years. The welfare rolls have been cut in half, and it isn't all a result of the good economy. It is churches getting busy and saying, "We are going to take care of the poor in our area." It is people changing their values and their attitudes toward work. Divorce is down 19 percent since 1981. Teenage pregnancies have been dropping steadily for the past five years. They are down 7.5 percent this past year. Abortions are down 15 percent since 1990.

And moral discourse is changing. A year ago, I appeared on one of these week-in-review, television programs, where the "talking heads" gather around a table and dispense all the wisdom from inside the Washington Beltway to all the masses outside the Beltway. I hate those programs, but the host was a friend whom I couldn't turn down. We got talking about the city of Washington. Toward the middle of the program, I ventured that I thought the problem of crime and the dissolution in the inner city was basically a moral problem.

Huh? There was an awkward silence. The host cleared his throat. Nobody said anything. (It seemed like a whole minute to me.) It was like I had come from another planet, talking about moral questions having something to do with our capital city! And then another panelist broke the silence, "Oh yes, Mr. Colson has a point. That is why we are building a new civic center here in D.C." They didn't get it!

But contrast that with the programs I have been on in the last seven or eight months—*Larry King* and *Nightline* and others—talking about whether private immorality has public consequences and talking about what repentance is.

This is no time to be talking about withdrawal and defeat, because moral discourse is changing in America. People are coming alive to the realization that something is wrong. I would like to say it is because of our preaching. I would like to say it is because of our moralistic crusades; but it isn't at all. They are realizing that what the "modern age" has believed in for much of the past century has failed them. With autonomy or free-choice being the exalted virtue of all virtues, they had been sure that we would find the Holy Grail. Instead, we found what we saw in Littleton, Colorado: that rebellion against God allows evil to come into the world.

> THIS IS NO TIME TO BE TALKING
> ABOUT WITHDRAWAL AND DEFEAT,
> BECAUSE MORAL DISCOURSE
> IS CHANGING IN AMERICA.

In Littleton we saw two world views in extraordinary contrast. Don't say ideas don't have consequences. In Littleton, young disciples of Nietzsche did exactly what Hitler did, only on a smaller scale. They believed the lie that God is dead and that we find our meaning through a world of power. They believed that, and they brought unspeakable evil into that high school. And yet God used that extraordinary moment to bring perhaps the most dramatic testimonies I have seen since I have been a Christian. Take Cassie Bernall and the others who gave such glowing testimonies. Cassie was a martyr. "Do you believe in God?" She said, "Yes." And she was shot. But have you ever seen anything on CNN like all of those televised memorial services? Jesus lifted up, reconciliation and healing and forgiveness! For at least a week, CNN looked like a Christian network. Amazing—two world views in sharp contrast and providing a powerful witness to what's gone terribly wrong and what's so very hopeful about the times in which we live.

The world has bought a lie—that you can be your own god; you can do what you want. But all of a sudden, people at the turn of this millennium are discovering that it simply doesn't work. We can't live with the moral nihilism that follows. We cannot live with the logical consequences of a flawed world view, because its own internal contradictions eventually catch up with us. People are now more worried, not about their own life choices, but about whether their kids will come home safe from school.

THE WORLD HAS BOUGHT A LIE— THAT YOU CAN BE YOUR OWN GOD; YOU CAN DO WHAT YOU WANT.

People are raising life-and-death questions, and this is the opportunity for us to walk forward boldly and say, "Yes, there is a better way." It is a reason we must not be tempted to withdraw from the culture.

Our Cultural Challenge

All of the experiments and great utopian visions of the twentieth century—none has provided viable and hopeful answers to the basic questions of life.

But there is a way, an answer. It is the time-honored way that you and I know: the gospel, the Good News. God created us, spoke us into existence; then we fell because we rebelled against His Word;

and yet He has redeemed us with the blood of His Son. This God gives us the opportunity to restore the culture that we live in.

As ministers of the gospel, you are not only to preach the Word, though, yes, you are to do that always in season and out of season, faithfully and truthfully. But you also are to take the Word of God and apply it to every single area of life. I have discovered that the more I am able to preach the Christian truth against the false values and beliefs of our culture, the more I am seeing skeptical and doubtful people begin to wake up. It is putting the gospel into a cultural context so that people can understand it, just as Paul did at Mars Hill.

If I walked into a room today and said, "Jesus is the answer," and the room was filled with Christians, they would nod and know what I meant. If they were Baptists like me, they would say, "Amen." But if I walked into a secular gathering and said, "Jesus is the answer," people would say, "What is the question?" We not only have to preach the answer, but we also have to tell them they have a question. And the good news is that they are beginning to discover that they have one. At the core of their beings, they know it.

I think this is a wonderful time to be in ministry. Go out and equip your flock so that every person in your church is a minister of the gospel, so that every person in your church can begin to change this culture in two ways, by living out the gospel and by contending for truth and challenging the false values of the culture.

If I have seen anything over the last twenty-five years in my own ministry, it is this: that while sometimes words fall flat, the world cannot deny the reality of the gospel when they see it lived out. When they see Prison Fellowship Angel Tree volunteers year after year taking Christmas gifts and the gospel to nearly half a million kids who have a parent in prison, and then mentoring many of them year 'round, the world says, "That is something different!"

The world says it when they see a prison like the InnerChange

Freedom Initiative in Texas, where Prison Fellowship is in charge of all prison programming, 'round the clock. I attended the graduation of one of the InnerChange classes last fall. I was standing there with about eight men who had successfully completed the eighteen months of in-prison training. As one prisoner, Ron Flowers, came to receive his certificate, I saw a tall, stately woman in the audience stand and walk forward. I knew who she was and was not surprised at what happened next, though many in the room were. After I gave Ron his certificate, she threw her arms around him and said, "This is Ron Flowers, my adopted son." Who was she? The mother of the woman Ron had murdered fourteen years earlier. He had denied his guilt right up until one month earlier when, on his knees during our program, he confessed his crime. The mother heard about it, came to the prison, and they were reconciled. That man is now out of prison and being mentored by the mother of the young woman he murdered. That is the gospel being lived out. People see that, and they can't deny the power of the gospel.

WE HAVE BEEN GIVEN A HOLY TRUST TO PROCLAIM AND DEFEND AND TAKE TO THE WORLD.

Even as you model living out your faith, train your flock and think about how you can challenge the false values of this culture. Remember, people are more open today than ever. I give a daily radio commentary called "BreakPoint" on which I tear down some of the false values of our secular society. One of the false values that I took on about a year ago was advertising, which often passes off a message that is about much more than a product. It is often promoting a philosophy or way of life. The Saab automobiles, for example, had an ad campaign: Drive a Saab and you "find your own road." Some of these ads were really antiestablishment. If you are the kind of person who tells your boss what to do with the job you don't like, if you are the kind of person who tells your boss off, you are the kind of person who ought to drive a Saab. I did a couple of radio programs on Saab ads and how they were promoting the existential philosophy of the sixties.

Well, I got a phone call a week later from the president of Saab U.S. (I said to my assistant, "You take that call.") But the guy was very persistent; he had to talk to me. "Mr. Colson, I heard your radio program," he said.

"Yes, I suspected you might."

"I want to tell you. We have been reviewing our ad campaign, and you made a very good point. I had never thought about it. We were selling a philosophy, not cars." He said, "You won't see those 'find your own road' ads anymore."

And I never did. They were dropped. You never see them. What's more, that man has subsequently become a friend.

We must break the world out of its shell, but to do so we have to have a biblically informed view of all of life. With God's help, we must embolden ourselves and recognize the truth that we have been given a holy trust to proclaim and defend and take to the world.

We have to be able to challenge these falsehoods ourselves; as ministers you must be able to equip your flocks and challenge them as well. This may mean equipping your flock to discuss these issues over the backyard grill and over the fence, because that is where cultures get changed as neighbor tells neighbor and neighbor tells neighbor. It will always bubble from the bottom up. Richard Lovelace taught me this. Great movements start from the bottom up. They don't come from the top down. Equip the flock to go out there. Little by little, piece by piece, in the classrooms, in the Rotary clubs, and in businesses, you begin to make a difference by showing people that the only rational way to order your life is in accordance with the moral and physical plan that God has given us for living. Nothing else works! And people are beginning to recognize this.

Our Millennial Opportunity

Why is this such a great opportunity? Look back at the last century. The century started in the era of post-Edwardian triumphalism. It was captured marvelously in the movie *Titanic*, which I saw on a transatlantic flight. (My pastor says no one should see it because there are nude scenes, but I'm okay—the version on the flight was edited.) There is an absolutely wonderful moment in that film when one of the British aristocrats in his finery is getting on the first-class cabin. He looks up at this marvelous vessel, and he says, "Ah! This is the ship that even God couldn't sink!" But, of course, it didn't finish its maiden voyage across the Atlantic. And post-Edwardian triumphalism lay in the blood-soaked mud of the trenches of Argonne in World War I.

Then we were seduced by Hegel to believe that Darwin's ideas of evolution would have social applications; if we just could evolve to higher states through knowledge and progress, we could usher in the utopian visions of the twentieth century. Nonsense!

Freud and Dewey greatly influenced us in this country by making us believe that the problems weren't in our own sinful nature but simply in the way we were nurtured and conditioned by society; we would be fine if we could change our influences and bring our true selves out. Tell that to the survivors of Auschwitz.

Then we believed the dreams of Marx, that we could throw off our chains: "Workers arise and be free!" In this past century, Marxism put two-thirds of the world into slavery.

We believed the modernists who told us that there was a naturalistic explanation for everything in the universe. Until the modern era, we accepted the premise that we had been created. But modernism has so completely failed that we now have postmodernism, which says that there is no truth at all; both God and reason fail, and thus we are left in a moral wasteland.

Go back through that century. Look at the teachings that have so influenced all of the utopian visions of this century right up to today. Go back and look at every single one of them, and what do you see? They are all on the ash heap of history. They have all been discredited. Modern man and modern woman look today at the dawn of the new millennium and have to realize that every single one of the utopian plans presented to us over the past century has been an utterly bankrupt failure.

That's the opportunity for us to step forward and to preach to them and to open their eyes by showing them the failure of their own way of life—to show them that there is a rational, coherent way to explain all the basic philosophical questions that have been asked from the beginning of time: *Where did I come from? Who am I? Why am I in this mess?* And is there a way out? Yes, as the new millennium dawns over the horizon, they will see the old rugged cross, the Truth of God's plan—"Jesus Christ the same, yesterday, today, and forever." They will see that that is the hope that we can bring to the world.

Yes, now is a time not for despair but for jubilation and excitement as we bring that kind of a message to a world that is ever more hungry for it.

God bless you as you do it. Preach that message. Don't miss the opportunity; don't "preach to the air." As Machen once put it: "Preach the truth straight." And by the power of the Spirit convict your congregations and other people you meet. And equip your flock with the Christian mind in order to defend that truth. God bless you in your ministries.

Harvard well deserves its reputation as a very liberal university—liberal in the best sense of the word—because you have as a lecturer in the university today someone who is an ex-convict.

Harvard also deserves the reputation for being a liberal university, in the best sense of the word, because over the last three years, I have written articles that here at Harvard could be considered quite impertinent, in which I have described my views on why it is impossible to teach ethics at Harvard. And you've invited me to speak anyway.

The Ethical Malaise

I'm no longer in politics. I've done my time, literally and figuratively. But it's awfully hard to watch what is happening on the political scene without a certain sense of dismay. Look at the Keating Five—five United States senators, tried, in effect, by their own tribunal. Just before that, Sen. Dave Durenberger, who happens to be a good friend of mine, was censured by the Senate. I also spent some time with Marion Barry, the former mayor of the District of Columbia, who was arrested for drug use. And in South Carolina and Arizona, scams in the legislatures have been exposed by federal prosecutors.

I saw a press release in which the Department of Justice boasted that in 1990 they had prosecuted and convicted 1,150 public officials, the highest number in the history of the republic. They were boasting about it, yet I read it with a certain sadness, because it seems that kind of corruption has become epidemic in American politics.

We have seen congressmen, one after another, Coehlo, Wright, Frank, Lukens—both sides of the aisle—either being censured or forced out of office. We see probably the most cynical scandal of all—the HUD scandal—where people were ripping off money from the public treasury that was designed to help the poor. Then we've seen more spy scandals during the past five years than in all previous years of American history combined—people selling their national honor for sexual favors or money.

Business is not immune. The savings and loan scandals are bad enough on the face of them, but the fact that they're so widespread has fostered almost a looter's mentality. Ivan Boesky, speaking at U.C.L.A. Business School in the 1980s said, "Greed is a good thing," and ended up spending three years in a federal prison. Recently one of the major pharmaceutical firms was fined ten million dollars for covering up violations of criminal statutes.

It affects athletics. Sugar Ray Leonard has just admitted to drug use. He's been a role model for lots of kids on the street. Pete Rose spent time in prison for gambling.

Academia has been affected. Stanford University's President Kennedy was charged with spending seven thousand dollars to buy a pair of sheets—they must be awfully nice bed linens—and charging them improperly to a government contract. One day, a Nobel Prize winner was exposed for presenting a fraudulent paper, and the very next day a professor at Georgetown University was charged with filing a fraudulent application for a grant from the National Institute of Health. Probably saddest of all, at least from my perspective, are the cases of certain religious leaders like Jimmy Swaggart and Jim Bakker. Bakker—whom I've visited in prison—was prosecuted for violating what should be the most sacred trust of all: to speak for God and to minister to people in their spiritual needs.

Are these simply examples of rotten apples or better prosecutors? Some people might dismiss these cases by saying, "This is simply the nature of humanity." I think it was Bishop Fulton Sheen, in paraphrasing G. K. Chesterton, who once said that the doctrine of original sin is the only philosophy empirically validated by thirty-five hundred years of human history. Maybe you dismiss this, too, and say, "This is just the way people are."

But is there a pattern here?

Time magazine, in its cover story on ethics, said what's wrong: "Hypocrisy, betrayal, and greed unsettle a nation's soul." The *Washington Post* said that the problem has reached the point where "common decency can no longer be described as common." The *New Republic* magazine said, "There is a destructive sense that nothing is true and everything is permitted."

I submit to you that when the *Washington Post,* the *New Republic* magazine, and *Time* magazine—which have never been known as bastions of conservative, biblical morality—begin to talk about some sort of ethical malaise, a line has been crossed. These aren't simply isolated instances, but rather a pattern emerging in American life.

No institution has been more sensitive to this than Harvard. Former President Bok has given some extraordinary speeches decrying the loss of ethics in the American business community. I think some of you have seen the recent polls finding that business school students across America, by a two-to-one margin, believe that businesses are generally unethical. It's a very fragile consensus that holds together trust in our institutions. When most business school students believe there aren't any ethical operations, you begin to wonder if something isn't affecting us a lot more broadly than isolated instances of misbehavior that have been exposed.

I believe we are experiencing today in our country what I choose to call a crisis of character: a loss of those inner restraints and virtues that prevent Western civilization from pandering to its own darker instincts.

If you look back through the history of Harvard, you'll see that President Elliott was as concerned about the development of character as he was about education. Plato once said, if you asked why we should educate someone, "we educate them so that they become a good person, because good persons behave nobly." I believe we should be deeply concerned about the loss of what Edmund Burke called the traditional values of republican citizenship—words like valor, honor, duty, responsibility, compassion, civility. Words that sound quaint when uttered in these surroundings.

The Path to Individualism

Why has this happened? Through twenty-three centuries of Western civilization, we were guided by a shared set of philosophical assumptions that there was a transcendent value system. This was not always the Judeo-Christian value system, though I think the Judeo-Christian values were, as the eminent historian Christopher Dawson wrote, "the heart and soul of Western civilization."

It goes back to the Greeks and Plato's saying that if there were no transcendent ideals, there could be no concord, justice, and harmony in a society. There is through twenty-three centuries of civilization—the history of the West—a strain of belief in a transcendent value system. Whether it was the unknown god of the Greeks, the Christ of the Scriptures revealed to the Christian, Yahweh of the Old Testament revealed to the Jew, or, as Enlightenment thinkers chose to call it, natural law—which I believe to be not inconsistent with Judeo-Christian revelation—this belief guided our conduct for twenty-three centuries until a great cultural revolution began in America.

I BELIEVE WE ARE EXPERIENCING TODAY IN OUR COUNTRY WHAT I CHOOSE TO CALL A CRISIS OF CHARACTER.

This revolution took place in our country in the 1960s. Some think it goes back further. Paul Johnson—who happens to be one of my favorite historians—wrote a history of Christianity, a history of the Jew, and a classic book called *Modern Times*. Johnson says that gradually, through the 1920s and 1930s, people began to challenge what had been the fixed assumptions by which people lived—the set of fixed and shared common values.

In the 1960s it exploded. The writings of Camus and Sartre invaded American campuses. Basically, they were what Camus said when he came to America and spoke at Columbia University in 1947. To the student body assembled he said, "There is nothing." The idea was introduced that there is no God. In this view there is no transcendent value; life is utterly meaningless, and the only way that we can derive meaning out of life is if we overcome the nothingness of life with heroic individualism. The goal of life is to overcome that nothingness and to find personal peace and meaning through your own autonomous efforts.

Most of the people of my generation dismissed what was happening on the campuses as a passing fad—as protest. It was not. The only people who behaved logically in the sixties were the flower children. They did exactly what they were taught; if there were no other object in life than to overcome the nothingness, then go out and smoke pot, make love, and enjoy personal peace.

Then America came through the great convulsion of Watergate and Vietnam—a dark era—and into the seventies. We thought we shook off those protest movements of the sixties. We did not; we simply embraced them into the mainstream of American culture. That's what gave rise to the "me" decade.

If you look at the best-sellers of the 1970s, they are very revealing: *Winning Through Intimidation, Looking Out for Number One,* and *I'm Okay, You're Okay.* Each of these was saying, "Don't worry about us." We emerged into a decade that Tom Wolfe, the social critic, called "the decade of me." Very logically, that graduated into the 1980s and what some have cynically called "the golden age of greed."

Sociologist Robert Bellah wrote a book titled *Habits of the Heart*—a phrase he borrowed from Tocqueville's classic work on American life. Bellah examined the values of several hundred average, middle-class Americans. He came to the conclusion that the reigning ethos in American life in the eighties was what he called "ontological individualism," a radical individualism where the individual is supreme and autonomous and lives for himself or herself. He found that Americans had two overriding goals: vivid personal feelings and personal success.

Bellah tried to find out what people expected from the institutions of society. From business, they expected personal advancement. Okay, that's fair enough. From marriage, personal development. No wonder marriages are in trouble. And from church, personal fulfillment! But the "person" became the dominant consideration.

I would simply say that this self-obsession destroys character. It has to! All of those quaint-sounding virtues I talked about, which historically have been considered the elements of character, are no match for a society in which the exaltation and gratification of self becomes the overriding goal of life.

Rolling Stone magazine surveyed members of the baby-boom generation. Forty percent said there was no cause for which they would fight for their country. If there's nothing worth dying for, there's nothing worth living for. The social contract unravels when that happens, and there can be no ethics.

The Pattern of the Normative

How can you then have ethical behavior? The crisis of character is totally understandable when there are no absolute values. The word *ethics* derives from the Greek word *ethos,* which literally meant *stall*—a hiding place. It was the one place you could go and find security. There could be rest and something that you could depend upon; it was immovable. Ethics or ethos is the normative; what ought to be.

Morals derives from the word *mores,* which means "always changing." *Morals* is what is rather than what ought to be. Unfortunately, in America today, we are guided by moral determinations. So we're not even looking at ethical standards. Ethical standards don't change; it's the stall; it's the ethos. But morals change all the time. So with shifting morals, if 90 percent of the people say that it's perfectly all right to do this, then that must be perfectly all right to do, because 90 percent of the people say it is. It's a very democratic notion.

Ethics is not—cannot be—democratic. *Ethics* by its very definition is authoritarian. That's a very nasty word to utter on any campus in America, and particularly at Harvard, where Arthur Schlesinger has written a magnificently argued assault on the perils of absolutism.

In a relativistic environment, ethics deteriorates to nothing more than utilitarian or pragmatic considerations. If you're really honest with yourselves and look at the ethical questions you're asked to wrestle with in classes, you will see that you are being taught how to arrive at certain conclusions yourself, and to make certain judgments yourself, which ultimately are going to be good for business. That's fine, and you should do that. That's a prudential decision that has to be made. That's being a responsible business leader. It just isn't ethics and shouldn't be confused with ethics.

Ethics is what ought to be, not what is or even what is prudential.

There was a brilliant professor at Duke University, Stanley Hauerwas, who wrote that "Moral life cannot be found by each person pursuing his or her options." In relativism, all you have is a set of options. The only way moral life can be produced is by the formation of virtuous people of traditional communities. That was the accepted wisdom of Western civilization until the cultural revolution of the sixties, with which we are still plagued.

What is the answer? I'd like to address two points: first, how each of us, individually, might view our own ethical framework, and second, why some set of transcendent values is vital.

We live in a pluralistic society. I happen to be a Baptist—and believe strongly that, in a pluralistic environment, I should be able to contend for my values as you should be able to contend for your values, and out of that contention can come some consensus we can all agree to live by. That's the beauty of pluralism. It doesn't mean extinguishing all ideas; it means contending for them and finding truth out of that consensus.

Out of the battle comes some consensus by which people live. But I would argue that there must be some values; and I would take the liberty of arguing for my belief in a certain set of historic values being absolutely essential to the survival of society.

Personal Issues

First, let me address the question of how we find it ourselves. If you studied philosophy as an undergraduate, you read about Immanual Kant and the categorical imperative. You read about rationalism and the ways in which people can find their own ethical framework. I guess the only thing I can tell you is that in my life—and I can't speak for anyone else—it didn't work.

I grew up in America during the Great Depression and thought that the great goal of life was success, material gain, power, and influence. That's why I went into politics. I believed I could gain power and influence how people live. If I earned a law degree—as I did at night—and accumulated academic honors and awards, it would enable me to find success, power, fulfillment, and meaning in life.

I had a great respect for the law. When I went through law school, I had a love for the law. I learned the history of jurisprudence and the philosophy underlying it.

I studied Locke, the Enlightenment, and social contract theories as an undergraduate at Brown, and had a great respect for the political process. I also had a well-above-average IQ and some academic honors. I became very self-righteous.

When I went to the White House, I gave up a law practice that was making almost two hundred thousand dollars a year (and that was back in 1969, which wasn't bad in those days). It's kind of ordinary now for graduates of Harvard Business School, but then it was a lot of money.

I had accumulated a little bit of money, so I took a job in the White House at forty thousand dollars a year. I took everything I had, and I stuck it in a blind trust at the Bank of Boston. Let me tell you, if you want to lose money, that's the surest way to do it! After three and a half years, when I saw what the Bank of Boston had done to my blind trust, I realized I was a lot poorer when I came out of the government than I was when I went into the government.

But there was one thing about which I was absolutely certain—that no one could corrupt me. Positive! And if anybody ever gave me a present at Christmastime, it went right to the driver of my limousine. They used to send in bottles of whiskey, boxes of candy, and all sorts of things that went right to the driver of my automobile. I wouldn't accept a thing.

Patty and I were taken out on someone's boat one day. I discovered it was a chartered boat and ended up paying for half of it, because I didn't want to give the appearance of impropriety. Imagine me, worried about such things!

THE GREATEST MYTH OF THE TWENTIETH CENTURY IS THAT PEOPLE ARE GOOD. WE AREN'T. WE'RE NOT MORALLY NEUTRAL.

I ended up going to prison. So much for the categorical imperative. The categorical imperative says that with our own rational process we will arrive at that judgment which, if everyone did it, would be prudential and the best decision for everyone. In other words, that which we would do, we would do only if we could will it to be a universal choice for everybody.

I really thought that way, and I never once thought I was breaking the law. I would have been terrified to do it, because I would jeopardize the law degree I had worked four years at night to earn. I had worked my way onto the Law Review, Order of the Coif, and Moot Court—all the things that lawyers do—and I graduated in the top of my class. I wouldn't put that in jeopardy for anything in the world.

I was so sure. But, you see, there are two problems. Every human being has an infinite capacity for self-rationalization and self-delusion. You get caught up in a situation where you are absolutely convinced that the fate of the republic rests on the reelection of, in my case, Richard Nixon. There's an enormous amount of peer pressure, and you don't take time to stop and think, *Wait a minute. Is this right by some absolute standard, or does this seem right in the circumstances? Is it okay?*

I was taught to think clearly and carefully. As a lawyer, that's what you do—you spend four years in law school, and you go like a monkey. You're briefing cases, briefing cases. We use the case method, as you use the case method here in business. The case method in law school, however, is a little bit different, because you always have a fixed conclusion; I knew there was a fixed law to arrive at. I had all the mental capacity to do that. And yet I was capable of infinite self-delusion.

Second, and even more important, which goes to the heart of the ethical dilemma in America today: Even if I had known I was doing wrong, would I have had the will to do what is right? It isn't hindsight. I tell you, the answer is no. The greatest myth of the twentieth century is that people are good. We aren't. We're not morally neutral.

My great friend Prof. Stan Samenow happens to be an orthodox Jew. I asked him one day, "Stan, if people were put in a room and no one could see what they were doing or no one knew what they were doing, would they do the right thing half the time and the wrong thing half the time? Would they do the wrong thing all the time, or would they do the right thing all the time?" He said they would always do the wrong thing.

We aren't morally neutral. I know that's a terribly unpopular thing to say in America today, but it happens to be true. The fundamental problem with learning how to reason through ethical solutions is that it doesn't give you a mechanism to override your natural tendency to do what is wrong. This is what C. S. Lewis—whose writings have had such a profound influence on my life—says.

My friend Tom Phillips gave me the book *Mere Christianity* when I came to him in the summer of 1973 at a moment of great anguish in my life. I wasn't so worried about what was going on in Watergate, but I knew I didn't like what was going on in my heart. But something was different about him. So I went to see him one evening.

I went, and that was the evening that this ex-marine captain, White House tough guy, Nixon hatchet man (and all kinds of things I was called in those days that you can't write about in print or wouldn't say in polite company—much of it justifiably) found myself unable to drive the automobile out of the driveway when I left his home, after he had told me of his experience with Jesus Christ. I was crying too hard.

I took that little book he had given me, *Mere Christianity*, and began to read it and study it as I would study for a case. I'd take my yellow legal pad and get down all the arguments—both sides. I was confronted with the most powerful mind that I had ever been exposed to. I saw the arguments for the truth of Jesus Christ, and I surrendered my life. My life has not been the same since and can never be the same again.

I discovered that Christ coming into your life changes your will. It gives you that will to do what you know is right, where even if you know what is right—and most of the time you won't—you don't have the will to do it. It's what C. S. Lewis wrote in that tremendous little book *The Abolition of Man*. I'd love for you to read *Mere Christianity*, but if you had to read just *Mere Christianity* or *The Abolition of Man* for today's cultural environment, read *The Abolition of Man*. Wonderful!

I don't know how to say this in language that is inclusive, but he wrote a marvelous essay called "Men Without Chests." It's a wonderful article about the will. He said the intellect can't control the passions of the stomach except by means of the will—which is the chest. But we mock honor—and then we are alarmed when there are traitors in our midst. It is like making geldings, he said, and then bidding them to multiply. He was talking about the loss of character in 1947 and 1948, long before the results we are witnessing today of the loss of character in American life.

Societal Issues: The Moral Impulse

What about society as a whole? Margaret Thatcher delivered what I consider to be one of the most remarkable speeches in modern times in the late 1980s before the Church of Scotland. You'll find it reprinted only in the *Wall Street Journal.* Margaret Thatcher said—and I'll paraphrase—that the truth of the Judeo-Christian tradition is infinitely precious, not only because she believes it is true (and she professed her own faith), but also because it provides the moral impulse that causes people to rise above themselves and do something greater than themselves, without which a democracy cannot survive. She went on to make the case—I think quite convincingly—that without Judeo-Christian values at the root of society, society simply can't exist.

Our founders believed this. We were not formed as a totally tolerant, neutral, egalitarian democracy. We were formed as a republic with a certain sense of republican virtue built into the citizenry, without which limited government simply couldn't survive. No one said it better than John Adams: "Our constitution was made only for a moral and religious people. It is wholly inadequate for the government of any other."

There are four ways in which that moral impulse works. Someone sent me a letter suggesting the topic for this speech, "Why

Good People Do Bad Things." I didn't have time to write back and say that I think it would be more appropriate to address "Why Bad People Do Good Things," because that's a more difficult question.

Why do we do good things? If we live in an age of ontological individualism, if radical individualism is the pervasive ethos of the day, if we simply live for the gratification of our senses, of our personal success, and vivid personal feelings, why do anything good? Who cares? It won't make a particle of difference unless it's important to your balance sheet. But that's pragmatism, that isn't doing good things. That's pure utilitarianism.

First, we do good things because there is something in us that calls us to something greater than ourselves.

Prison Fellowship is, of course, a ministry in the prisons—not a very glamorous place to be. I visited three prisons this weekend. I was so moved in one prison because there were six hundred inmates who came out and saw their lives change. Those were people who were lost and forgotten. One man stood up and said, "Ten years ago I was in the prison and two of your volunteers, a couple, came in, Mr. Colson, and they befriended me." He said, "You know, they've been visiting me every month and writing to me ever since, for ten years."

Why do people do things like this? Why do they go to the AIDS wards? One of my friends goes into the AIDS ward of a prison all of the time, and people die in his arms. Do we do it because we have some good instinct? No! It is a moral impulse.

Why did William Wilberforce stand up on the floor of the Parliament in the House of Commons and denounce the slave trade? He said it was barbaric, and his courage cost him the prime ministership of England! "But," he said, "I have no choice as a Christian." He spent the next twenty years battling the slave trade and brought it to an end in England because of his Christian conscience.

What is it that makes us, as otherwise self-centered people

disposed to evil (if the history of the twentieth century and civilization is correct), what is it that makes us do good?

Second, Margaret Thatcher is absolutely right. A society cannot survive without a moral consensus.

I tell you this as one who sat next to the president of the United States and observed our nation's fragile moral consensus during the Vietnam era. We did some excessive things, and we were wrong. But we did it feeling that if we didn't, the whole country was going to fall apart. It was like a banana republic having the Eighty-Second Airborne down in the basement of the White House. One night, my car was firebombed on the way home. They had 250,000 protesters in the streets. You almost wondered if the White House was going to be overrun.

The moral consensus that holds our country together was in great peril during that era and during the entire Watergate aftermath of Vietnam. A free society can't exist without it.

Now, what gives it to us? Thomas Aquinas wrote that without moral consensus, there can be no law. Chairman Mao gave the other side of that in saying that morality begins at the muzzle of a gun. Every society has two choices: whether it wants to be ruled by an authoritarian ruler, or whether there can be a set of shared values and certain things we hold in common that give us the philosophical underpinnings of our value system in our life.

I submit to you that without that—call it natural law, if you wish, call it Judeo-Christian revelation, call it the accumulated wisdom of twenty-three centuries of Western civilization—I don't believe a society can exist.

The reason we have the most terrible crime problem in the world in America today is simple: We've lost our moral consensus. We're people living for ourselves.

We doubled the prison population in America during the 1980s.

We are, today, number one in the rate of incarceration per capita in the world. When I started Prison Fellowship in 1976, the U.S. was number three. We trailed the Soviet Union and South Africa. Today we're number one. While we build more prisons and put more people in, the recidivism rate remains constant at 74 percent. When prisoners are released, those people go right back to crime and prison again.

The answer to it is very simple. There are kids being raised today in broken families who are not being given values. Remember that Stanley Hauerwas said the way you foster ethics is in tradition-formed communities. They're not being given values in the home; they're not being given values in the school; they're watching the television set for seven hours and thirty-six minutes a day; and what they're seeing is, "you only go around once, so grab for all the gusto you can." Now if that's the creed by which you live, then at twelve years old, you're out on the streets sniffing coke. We arrest them and put them in jail. They think we're crazy. So do I.

Until you have some desire in society to live by a different set of values, we'll be building prisons until, as is the case today, 25 percent of the black, male inner-city population in America is either in prison or on probation or parole. We can't make it without that moral consensus. It will cost us dearly if we can't find a way to restore it.

Prof. James Wilson, formerly at Harvard Law School, wrote one of the most telling pieces I've ever read, and I refer to it in my book *Kingdoms in Conflict*. He wrote a very interesting primer about the relationship between spiritual values and crime. The prevailing myth is that crime goes up during periods of poverty. Actually, it went down during the 1930s. He found that during periods of industrialization crime went up, as what he called "Victorian values" began to fade. When there was a resurgence of spiritual values, crime went down. He saw a direct correlation. Crime went up whenever spiritual values went down; when spiritual values went up, crime went down.

Third, I think we in America often miss the basis of sound policy because we have become secularized in our views and afraid to look at biblical revelation. We're terrified of it.

When Ted Koppel gave the commencement speech at Duke University a few years ago, in which he said the Ten Commandments weren't the Ten Suggestions, and that God handed the Commandments to Moses at Mt. Sinai, you know what the press did to him. It was horrible. A fellow like Ted Koppel couldn't possibly say something like that! So we often blind ourselves to what can be truth.

CRIME WENT UP WHENEVER SPIRITUAL VALUES WENT DOWN; WHEN SPIRITUAL VALUES WENT UP, CRIME WENT DOWN.

I have spoken to state legislatures and with many other political leaders around this country. I always make the same argument to them about our prisons. We have way too many people in prison. Half of them are in for nonviolent offenses, which to me is ludicrous. They should be put to work. People should not be sitting in a cell doing nothing, at a cost to taxpayers of twenty thousand dollars a year, while their victims get no recompense. Offenders ought to be put in a work program to pay back their victims. Whenever I speak about that, the response I get from political officials is amazing.

In the Texas legislature, I gave that talk, and they applauded. Afterward, the speaker of the House said, "Mr. Colson, wait here. I'm sure some of the members would like to talk to you." They came flooding in afterward. They all said that restitution was a wonderful idea; where did that come from? I asked, "Have you got a Bible at home? Go home and dust it off, and you'll see that's exactly what God told Moses on Mt. Sinai."

That's biblical truth. That's the lesson of Jesus and Zacchaeus. We blind ourselves to it. In today's tolerant society, we think there's something wrong with ancient biblical truth. But in a pluralistic society, we ought to be seeking out wisdom. If we can find wisdom, find it. So often we find wisdom in the teachings of the Holy Scriptures.

Fourth, no society exists in a vacuum. Vacuums don't remain vacuums; they get filled. In a vacuum, a tyrant will often emerge. You've just seen seventy years of that crumble in the former Soviet Union. Isn't it interesting that when it crumbles, it so often crumbles because people have an allegiance to a power above the power of that earthly potentate?

I remember when Pope John Paul II said that he would return to Poland if the Soviets invaded during Poland's period of martial law in the early eighties. Years earlier, Stalin had said, "Hah! The Pope! How many divisions does he have?" Well, as a result of the Solidarity movement, we saw how many divisions he had—a whole lot more than the Soviets.

In 1981 I boarded a plane and came up to Boston to see our first grandson when he was born. A man got up in the aisle of the plane, all excited to see me. He said, "Chuck Colson!" He was talking so fast I could hardly understand him. He introduced himself as Benigno Aquino and said that when he'd been in jail for seven years and seven months, as a political prisoner of Marcos, he had read my book *Born Again*. In a prison cell, he had gotten down on his knees and surrendered his life to Jesus Christ. After that, he said, his entire experience in prison changed.

Nino and I became pretty good friends. We did some television programs together, and we visited frequently. He called me up one day and said, "I'm going back to the Philippines." I said, "Nino, do you think that's wise?" He said, "I have to. I am going back, because my conscience will not let me do otherwise." He was safe here in America. He had a fellowship at Harvard, and he could lecture anywhere he wanted. He and his wife had everything they could possibly want.

But he knew he had to go back to the Philippines. "My conscience will not let me do otherwise." He said, "If I go to jail, it'll be okay; I'll be president of Prison Fellowship in the Philippines. If there are free elections, I'll be elected president. I know I can beat Marcos. And if I'm killed, I know I'll be with Jesus Christ." He went back in total freedom. And he was shot and killed as he got off the airplane.

But an extraordinary thing happened—what's known as people power. People went out into the streets. The tanks stopped. People went up and put flowers down the muzzles of guns. A tyrant was overthrown. A free government was reasserted, because people believed in a power above themselves.

I was in the former Soviet Union last year and visited five prisons, four of which had never been visited by anyone from the West. I met with Soviet officials, including Vadim Bakatin, then minister of interior affairs. When talking about the enormous crime problem in the Soviet Union, he said to me, "What are we going to do about it?" I said, "Mr. Bakatin, your problem is exactly the one that Fyodor Dostoyevsky, your great novelist, diagnosed. In *Brothers Karamazov,* he had that debate between the older brother, who is unregenerate, and the younger brother, Alexis, who is the priest, over the soul of the middle brother, Ivan. At one point, Ivan yells out and says, "Ah, if there is no God, everything is permissible." Crime becomes inevitable. I said, "Your problem in the Soviet Union is seventy years of atheism." He said, "You're right. We need what you're talking about. How do we get it back in the Soviet Union?"

All I could think was how foolish we are in America to be squandering our heritage. In a country where they've ignored the King of greater power for seventy years, they're losing it all.

Summary

I leave you with a very simple message, as someone who had thought he had it all together and attained a position of great power. I never thought I'd be one of the half dozen men sitting around the desk of the president of the United States, with all of that power and influence. I discovered that there was no restraint on the evil in me. In my self-righteousness, I was never more dangerous.

I discovered what Solzhenitsyn wrote so brilliantly from a prison— that the line between good and evil passes not between principalities and powers, but it oscillates within the human heart. Even the most rational approach to ethics is defenseless if there isn't the will to do what is right. On my own—and I can speak only for myself—I do not have that will. That which I want to do, I do not do; that which I do, I do not want to do.

It's only when I can turn to the One whom we celebrate at Easter—the One who was raised from the dead—that I can find the will to do what is right. It's only when that value and that sense of righteousness pervade a society that there can be a moral consensus. I would hope I might leave with you, as future business leaders, the thought that a society of which we are a part—and for which you should have a great sense of responsibility and stewardship—desperately needs those kind of values. And, if I might say so, each one of us does as well.

Personal Integrity and Public Service

Geneva College
Beaver Falls, Pennsylvania
Commencement, 1998

In an earlier age, the question at hand might have sounded a bit absurd: Does character matter, and does it have anything to do with public service?

As recently as a generation ago, I can't imagine anyone giving a college commencement address on this subject, because education was considered to be not only the acquisition of knowledge but also the formation of moral character. That's what education was all about. That is why the president of Harvard University, until the middle of the nineteenth century, taught courses in ethics. Every college started in America before the twentieth century—with the exception of the University of South Carolina—was originally founded by Christians. Even when I was at Brown in the 1950s, attending chapel was mandatory. Can you imagine that from such a liberal bastion today? How dramatically things have changed.

We have taken the moral component out of education and culture. President Teddy Roosevelt said that "to educate a man in the mind and not in morals, is to educate a menace to society." Thank God for Christian institutions like Geneva College that still care about educating people not only in the mind, but also in the conscience—providing moral education and formation.

"TO EDUCATE A MAN IN THE MIND AND NOT IN MORALS, IS TO EDUCATE A MENACE TO SOCIETY."

Brave New World?

The moral decline in our country has not been limited to college campuses; we see it throughout the culture. Remember the so-called ethical malaise of the 1980s, the Decade of Greed, the Wall Street scandals, Milken, Boesky, and other names that are now legend? Americans and the media went after them with a vengeance, because we knew something was wrong. There was a concern for the ethics of the nation. The *Washington Post* said, "We've reached the point where common decency can no longer be described as common." *Time* magazine characterized the era as one of "hypocrisy, betrayal, greed, and unsettled emotions." We were deeply concerned in the eighties with the question of ethics and moral behavior. In Clarence Thomas's confirmation hearings for the Supreme Court, many of the objections to him focused on matters of personal ethics, not on the job he had done. The media made the argument that issues of character, his personal character, had considerable relevance to what kind of Supreme Court justice he would be. The partisanship and nature of the attacks on him notwithstanding, that was a valid line of reasoning. Whether or not the Senate panel was sincere in its questioning, consideration of his personal integrity was a valid question. Sen. John Tower, who happened to be a friend of mine, was nominated to be secretary of defense and was denied the nomination because of charges of womanizing and drinking. Perhaps rightly so. Bob Packwood, with a long, distinguished, and effective career in the U.S. Senate, was driven out of that body for unseemly behavior toward women—rightly so, in my opinion.

But what has happened just a decade later, in the nineties? Please understand this point without partisanship, because I would say this regarding a president who was a Republican just as well as a Democrat. If you follow the polls in response to the Clinton White House scandal, personal character and integrity are considered to have absolutely no relevance to public service. If the charges that have been made concerning the president are true, if there is any validity whatsoever, to dismiss them out of hand marks a true turn in the American political and social landscape. Two-thirds of the American people seem to say that if indeed the president of the United States has committed perjury, suborned perjury, tampered with witnesses, and committed a series of sexual indiscretions, it should make no political difference, because the country is doing so well.

At the same time, a poll indicates that 97 percent of the American people believe that their own moral behavior is superior to that of the president. It seems as if a spaceship has suddenly flown over this country and dropped some desensitizing nerve gas upon us.

The effect is that everybody's moral nerve endings have been totally numbed; it's as if we don't care. It's as if character means nothing, as if it's okay to do anything you want to do.

For summer reading, I suggest you open Aldous Huxley's *Brave New World*, written in the late 1930s. Huxley turned out to be the great prophet of the latter half of the twentieth century (not Orwell with his futuristic *1984,* as we believed). Huxley suggested that people could be amused into submission, so that the controllers of the state could rule over us once everyone had been given free sex and soma, a little pill that would make everyone feel good on all occasions. The implication was that if you can make people feel good, they wouldn't care about anything else. God forbid that this has happened to us. If it has, we must appreciate what a dangerous concept this is to our body politic.

Our country's founding fathers would be appalled to know we were framing the day's political debate in this way. Our government was never established to be a democracy. It was established to be a republican—or representative—form of government in which leaders are elected (or appointed with authority to govern). They are to represent the people. Members of the United States Senate, for example, were never to be elected directly, but rather appointed by the state representatives. That's why we still have the Electoral College, something most people think is an anachronism. But it is not, or it shouldn't be. In principle, it gathers together those who know the candidates best, and they cast the votes. In this way the public officials would be somewhat removed from the current passions and whims of the masses. The point of this was to see that leaders need not be subjected to public passion—or polls. They were expected to use their good judgment to do what was truly good and truly in the best interests of the people, not necessarily what some poll told them the people wanted on a particular day.

We've totally abandoned that notion. We've given up on the idea that our public officials should be men and women, as Benjamin Franklin put it, of wisdom and character and virtue. Our founding fathers presupposed that our leaders would be people of virtue, because that's the only way self-government can possibly survive; otherwise we'd need police to enforce everything. John Adams said that our Constitution was made only for a religious people; for any other kind, it must be considered wholly inadequate.

Michael Novak says it so pointedly. He says a society of Americans that exalts virtue has 270 million policemen—individual consciences; a society that mocks virtue can't hire enough. And you know what happens to a society that can't hire enough police. The Germans, the Italians, the Japanese, and the Russians found out.

Age-Old Justice

Let me turn to a pertinent philosophical question. What were Socrates and his interlocutors trying to discover in *The Republic,* Plato's great classic of philosophy, which he wrote to answer the question: What is justice? Socrates zeroes in on the question we all might ask: Is it better to appear just or to be just? If you read *The Republic,* you know Socrates's great story of the ring of Gyges. Gyges finds this ring that allows him to become invisible and get away with anything he wants. Ultimately this ability allows him to steal the king's throne and the king's wife. Above all, Gyges seeks to serve his own interest. Socrates asks if it is just for Gyges to do what he can get away with so long as in the process he is able to appear righteous to the rest of society.

America today does not seem to ask itself that question: Is it just and right? Instead, we ask, "How has Gyges handled the economy?" "How are our mutual funds doing under the reign of the illegitimate King Gyges?" We've lost what has been a fundamental political question that people have asked throughout history: What is justice? Is it better to be just or merely to appear just? Think of it. Everything you do in your life, every single decision you make, ask yourself: Is it better to appear righteous or to be righteous? If you answer that question properly, I believe you can live lives of nobility, decency, and character, and you will contribute something of worth to your society and to your culture.

Character and Integrity

What is character? Character is a neutral word. The character of a podium might be that it is made of wood—or of metal. A person's character can be exemplary or disgraceful. The question is whether we care about good character. Do we care about being the kind of person who acts according to what he knows to be true in his heart, not according to how he will be perceived? The kind of person who believes in truth, justice, nobility, and honesty? Or are we the kind of people who accept lies and are self-serving, dishonest, and given to the baser passions? Every society, up until now, has always exalted virtue and said that bad character is something to be discouraged, that the baser passions must be restrained. It seems we no longer care.

Lost: Esteem for Virtue

Why do we no longer esteem virtue in our public servants? Why has this happened?

First, in our culture we have witnessed in the last thirty years a systematic erosion of the belief in truth. Seventy-two percent of the American people say there is no such thing as absolute truth. But there is absolute truth. Jesus Himself said, "I am the truth" (see John 14:6). There is ultimate reality. God has created us; God has spoken.

There is a known physical order, and there is a known moral order, because God has created it, even in a society that says there is no such thing. It's true. And if there is truth to be known, each of us has the capacity to know what is right and what is wrong. If you can't define what is right and wrong, then you are headed for the kind of moral nihilism so prevalent today. Samuel Johnson, the great

British writer, once was told that a guest coming to his home for dinner believed morality was a sham. Johnson countered, "If he believes there's no difference between virtue and vice, then let us be sure to count the spoons before he leaves."

The Chronicle of Higher Education reports some of the more terrifying things that students say when they are asked whether or not something can be absolutely right. John Leo uses the word *absolutophobia* to describe this inability of students to label anything objectively true or false, good or bad. College students in America today are unwilling to say categorically that the Nazi atrocities were wrong. We've come that far in our relativistic culture.

> THERE IS A KNOWN PHYSICAL ORDER, AND THERE IS A KNOWN MORAL ORDER, BECAUSE GOD HAS CREATED IT, EVEN IN A SOCIETY THAT SAYS THERE IS NO SUCH THING.

Second, we've lost any sense of true distinction between vice and virtue. We've raised a generation without conscience. This is something I come face-to-face with in my work in the prisons. I look into the cold eyes of young felons and understand why tragic shootings in Jonesboro and Paducah happened, and why in Pittsburgh recently a student walked into school and shot his teacher. I understand why kids in Central Park in New York cut apart somebody they just stumbled upon in the middle of the night. These kids disemboweled him and disfigured his face. People in the past have attributed such acts to poverty or to kids being minorities—that's nonsense. These were all white kids and all from upper-middle-class neighborhoods and families. Don't tell me social-economic reasons were to blame. Kids commit horrible crimes because we haven't informed and instructed their consciences, because we've abandoned virtue, and because we've said character doesn't matter. These kids are beginning to believe that. We've begun to confuse celebrity and fame with virtue, so that there is no difference between a Dennis Rodman and a Reggie White. There's no difference between somebody who gives his money to the poor and tries to help people in need, as Reggie White does, and someone who makes a complete fool out of himself as a public spectacle. In fact, we may even praise the fool above the principled man if that principled man stirs up controversy by speaking forcefully about biblical morality.

The third appalling thing we've said is that what we do with our bodies doesn't matter. Think about this. In the last thirty years, we've embarked upon an experiment in this country, largely fueled by the sexual revolution and the idea that sexual freedom is the highest enshrined constitutional right. We've said that what we do with our bodies has nothing to do with our real selves. It's a modern dualism. We have separated what every culture has believed to be as one. This new dualism says that the body is simply an instrument we can use in any way we want.

The Christian doctrine is totally opposite of that; the body, soul, and spirit are united as a whole. The body is part of us and is so valuable to God that it will be resurrected on judgment day when He returns. It is so vital that marriage is considered a covenant relationship in which two bodies come together and make one flesh. Well, it's no surprise we've abandoned that. We say that the body is like an automobile; I can get in it and drive it and take it anyplace, using it for pleasure and simply doing anything I want. We're rather cavalier about this, but this dualism leads to absolute destruction.

Does this pose any practical difficulty? People may have a poor understanding of the nature of the human being, but does it really matter? Yes it does. In separating the individual into these instrumental parts—mind, body, and spirit—we disintegrate the parts, and disintegrated people cannot form integrated relationships with others. Disintegrated people create disintegrated society. That's precisely what we have done.

Found: Personal Integrity and Character

This leads us to the question of integrity. Integrity is wholeness, the opposite of the disintegration of which I speak about. Anyone who's ever been in the navy knows about integrity. Remember what happens when a naval ship sets sail? Someone goes up to the captain on the bridge, and the captain says, "Check for watertight integrity." Someone goes down through the ship and checks every single door to see that every waterproof door is secured. The sailor goes back up to the captain to report that the ship has watertight integrity. Integrity means every hatch is closed—no leaks anywhere in your life. Integrity concerns every single part of your existence at sea. Falling short in any area destroys the wholeness. When we see this, we understand why private actions have public consequences. To think otherwise is like opening one of those watertight doors. That ship will eventually sink. Someone who will cheat in private is a cheater. Someone who lies in private is a liar and will likely lie in public. You can't give your trust, public or private, to someone who does that.

I leave you with a possibly radical thought, though who would have thought we would reach the point in America where this would be considered radical? I want you to go out into the world not only as men and women who are educated, but also as people who strive all your lives to develop integrity, character, purity, and virtue. In your families. In your businesses. In all your relationships. I want your lives to make a difference by the moral examples you provide through your actions.

I was a marine officer. There I realized that when you're preparing to go into combat, the most important thing is that the fellow in the next foxhole—on whom you depend when the shooting begins—is indeed dependable when the shooting begins. I cared a whole lot more about the character of that marine than I did his IQ, because my life would absolutely depend on his character if we got into battle. As you go through life, whether it's in the military, in your businesses, in your churches, or whatever walk of life (and certainly in your family), someone is going to depend on your character more than upon your IQ.

Build and develop your character. It's essential to us; it's essential to freedom. How do you do it?

For an answer, I turn to Scripture, the greatest message of all:

"Whoever can be trusted with very little can also be trusted with much" (Luke 16:10 NIV).

"Show proper respect to everyone" (1 Pet. 2:17 NIV).

"Speaking the truth in love. . ." (Eph. 4:15 NIV).

"Simply let your 'Yes' be 'Yes,' and your 'No,' 'No' " (Matt. 5:37 NIV).

"Act justly [do justice] and love mercy and walk humbly with your God" (see Micah 6:8).

"Whatever is true, whatever is noble, whatever is right, whatever is pure, whatever is lovely, whatever is admirable—if anything is excellent or praiseworthy—think about such things" (Phil. 4:8 NIV).

"Fear God and keep his commandments, for this is the whole duty of man" (Eccl. 12:13 NIV).

"Who may live on your holy hill? He whose walk is blameless and who does what is righteous, who speaks the truth from his heart and has no slander on his tongue, who does his neighbor no wrong and casts no slur on his fellowman, who despises a vile man but honors those who fear the LORD, who keeps his oath, his word, even when it hurts. . ." (Ps. 15:1–4 NIV).

"Stop doing wrong, learn to do right! Seek justice, encourage the oppressed. Defend the cause of the fatherless, plead the case of the widow" (Isa. 1:16–17 NIV).

SUBJECTIVISM OF VALUES IS ETERNALLY INCOMPATIBLE WITH DEMOCRACY.

Fifty years ago, at age fifty, C. S. Lewis saw clearly what was happening in Western culture with the emergence of relativism and the loss of confidence in moral truth. This is what he wrote in an article entitled "The Poison of Subjectivism": "The very idea of freedom presupposes some objective moral law, which overarches rulers and ruled alike. Subjectivism of values is eternally incompatible with democracy. We and our rulers are of one kind only so long as we are subject to one law, but if there is no law of nature, the ethos of any society is the creation of its rulers, educators, and [a wonderful word he uses] conditioners. Unless we return to the crude and nursery-like belief in objective values, we perish."

My single message to you is "do your duty." In the darkest days of Watergate, I was converted to Christ. Every day when I get up in the morning, I thank God for that moment when I realized my own sin was taken from me and knew that, as a historical fact, the Son of God went to the cross in order to set me free. That night twenty-five years ago, I—the toughest of the Nixon tough guys, the White House hatchet man—realized what was in my heart. What I saw was not the stuff you read about in Watergate reports, but much worse. And I tell you, I would suffocate in the stench of my own sins today if I did not know that Christ took them away. That night I realized the truth that I could be set free. What does that do to me? That inspires in me what G. K. Chesterton said was the "mother of all virtues": gratitude. Because of my gratitude, I will do for my God whatever He calls me to do.

And what He calls us to do is to live for Him in biblical fidelity to the kinds of commands found in Scripture, cited above. He calls us to be men and women of character who exalt virtue, who go into a society that has disdained character and mocks virtue and be light to a darkened world. We will confront what the world has to offer and stand firm, all the while saying, "We believe in truth, and we're going to live the right way, no matter what the cost."

Be that kind of men and women. God bless you.